"THIS
IS
LIFE
ETERNAL"

"THIS IS LIFE ETERNAL"

Mark E. Petersen

BOOKCRAFT
Salt Lake City, Utah

Library of Congress Catalog Card Number: 82-83633
ISBN O-88494-474-3

First Printing, 1982

Lithographed in the United States of America
PUBLISHERS PRESS
Salt Lake City, Utah

Contents

He Points the Way

Early in his ministry, the Apostle Peter defended the Lord and the gospel of Jesus Christ when he was called before the rulers, elders, and scribes in Jerusalem.

An impotent man had been healed at the gates of the temple. The rulers demanded:

"By what power, or by what name, have ye done this?

"Then Peter, filled with the Holy Ghost, said unto them, Ye rulers of the people, and elders of Israel,

"If we this day be examined of the good deed done to the impotent man, by what means he is made whole;

"Be it known unto you all, and to all the people of Israel, that by the name of Jesus Christ of Nazareth, whom ye crucified, whom God raised from the dead, even by him doth this man stand here before you whole.

"This is the stone which was set at nought of you builders, which is become the head of the corner.

"Neither is there salvation in any other: for there is none other name under heaven given among men, whereby we must be saved." (Acts 4:8-12.)

Not only was this a vital message to the rulers of the Jews, but also to all mankind:

"Neither is there salvation in any other: for there is none other name under heaven given among men, whereby we must be saved."

Jesus Himself had said: "By me if any man enter in, he shall be saved." (John 10:9.) But "by me"!

The Apostle Paul made it clear to the Ephesians that there is but one way to be saved—there is but one God, one Savior, the Lord Jesus Christ, who gave us but one "faith" or gospel and one baptism, with no variations. No man has the right to change the things of God. (Ephesians 4:4-14.)

When he wrote to the Galatians, he made it clear to them, as they left the gospel of Christ for "another gospel which is not another," that there is only one. "But," he said, "there be some that trouble you and would pervert the gospel of Christ." (Galatians 1:6-7.)

He felt so strongly about this that he called down a curse upon anyone who taught doctrines different from those of the true gospel.

"Though we, or an angel from heaven, preach any other gospel unto you than that which we have preached unto you, let him be accursed.

"As we said before, so say I now again, if any man preach any other gospel unto you than that ye have received, let him be accursed." (Galatians 1:8-9.)

And yet, the history of Christianity has been one of apostasy, of revisions of the word of God by uninspired men, of writing new and conflicting creeds, and of abandonment of some doctrines and ordinances of Christ.

Based on their man-made creeds, some say that any church will do, that all roads lead to Rome. And yet Christ organized but one church. He pleaded for unity among the members. Do we remember how Paul fought schisms in the Church, how he denounced divisions and apostasy?

"Is Christ divided?" he demanded of the Corinthians. "I beseech you brethren, by the name of our Lord Jesus Christ, that ye all speak the same thing, and that there be no divisions among you; but that ye be perfectly joined together in the same mind and in the same judgment." (1 Corinthians 1:13, 10.)

An earnest seeker for the truth will want to know which of all the hundreds of conflicting creeds is right, and which church to join. How can he tell which way to go?

The true Church of Jesus Christ as established in ancient times by the Lord and His apostles had definite marks of identification which may direct anyone to the truth.

It must be remembered, however, that all parts must be fitly joined together to make the whole, as Paul said. What are some of those marks of identification?

We mention but a few, as there are many.

1. The true church must declare the revealed facts about the nature of God, and teach Him as a Person, glorified and celestialized, after whose *physical* form mankind was made. "In our image, after our likeness." (Genesis 1:26.)

2. It must acknowledge Jesus Christ of Nazareth as the *divine* Son of God, the Savior, Redeemer, and Creator.

3. It must be headed by living apostles and prophets, with Jesus Christ Himself as the chief cornerstone.

4. It must have in it current revelation, for how could God guide His Church otherwise?

5. Its ministers must be called of God as was Aaron.

6. Salvation is provided through it for the dead as well as for the living. This includes preaching the gospel to the dead in the spirit world, and the performance of saving ordinances for them here, vicariously, the living acting for the dead.

7. The true church will produce new and additional scripture as the living prophets record their revelations and other dealings with the Lord.

8. Baptism is required to fulfill all righteousness, as the Lord Himself said. It is for the remission of sins. It must be by immersion to fit the symbolism of the burial and resurrection of the Savior. It must be performed by proper authority.

9. The Holy Ghost must be conferred upon baptized people by the laying on of hands of those in authority.

10. It must recognize that a worldwide apostasy from the original Church has taken place, in fulfillment of prophecy, as a preliminary to the Second Coming of Christ.

11. It must be a restored church—brought back by angelic ministry in the hour of God's judgment. Hence it must be a strictly modern church, headed by present-day apostles and prophets guided by current revelation.

Many other examples might be given. This book attempts to explain some details by which anyone may know the truth and be saved by seeking and accepting the one true Church of Jesus Christ. That is why this book was written.

Chapter One

The One Sheepfold

The Savior is the Good Shepherd, and He likens His followers to sheep in His fold. Of that fold He said:

"I am the door: by me, if any man enter in, he shall be saved, and shall go in and out and find pasture. . . .

"I am the good shepherd: the good shepherd giveth his life for the sheep. . . . I lay down my life for the sheep." (John 10:9, 11, 15.)

All are invited to enter the sheepfold. But although invited, they must come in His own way. Another way — any other way — is not acceptable to Him. He firmly declared:

"Verily, verily I say unto you, He that entereth not by the door into the sheepfold, but climbeth up some other way, the same is a thief and a robber." (John 10:1.)

And what is His sheepfold? It is His Church wherein His sheep are taught to live so that they may become like Him. His Church is the means of achieving "the perfecting of the saints, for the work of the ministry, for the edifying of the body of Christ." (Ephesians 4:12.)

His Church, or the body of its members, is likened to His own body. The Apostle Paul told the Ephesians that God "put all things under his (Christ's) feet, and gave him to be the head over all things to the church, *which is his body."* (Ephesians 1:22-23. Italics added.)

When Paul further referred to the members and the Church organization, he said that the whole body must be "fitly joined together and compacted by that which every joint supplieth." (Ephesians 4:16.)

Note the use of the word "compacted." When Paul wrote to the Corinthians on the same subject, he devoted a full chapter to it. He made the following points:

"For the body is not one member, but many. If the foot shall say, Because I am not the hand, I am not of the body; is it therefore not of the body? And if the ear shall say, Because I am not the eye, I am not of the body; is it therefore not of the body?

"If the whole body were an eye, where were the hearing? If the whole were hearing, where were the smelling? But now hath God set the members every one of them in the body, as it hath pleased him.

"And if they were all one member, where were the body? But now are they many members, yet but one body. And the eye cannot say unto the hand, I have no need of thee; nor again the head to the foot, I have no need of you.

"Nay, much more those members of the body, which seem to be more feeble, are necessary: And those members of the body, which we think to be less honourable, upon these we bestow more abundant honour; and our uncomely parts have more abundant comeliness.

"For our comely parts have no need: but God hath tempered the body together, having given more abundant honour to that part which lacked." (1 Corinthians 12:14-24.)

Laying down this important principle, Paul then affirms:

"That there should be no schism in the body; but that the members should have the same care one for another." (1 Corinthians 12:25.)

This was a reflection of Christ's own teachings while He was yet on earth. He emphasized *oneness and unity!*

When He prayed in behalf of His followers—His own Church members—He appealed to the Father for unity on their part and asked "that they all may be one; as thou, Father, art in me, and I in thee, that they also may be one in us: that the world may believe that thou hast sent me." (John 17:21.)

Two great principles are involved in that verse: first, the members must be united, for there can be no division in Christ, and second, their very oneness should be a converting factor, "that the world may believe that thou hast sent me."

Would the world be converted by conflict within the ranks? No wonder Paul said there should be no schism among the disciples.

The command of the Lord is for unity. Keeping that in mind we recall that He said:

"If a man love me, he will keep my words. . . . he that loveth me not keepeth not my sayings." (John 14:23-24.)

Paul continued his letter to the Corinthians:

"Now ye are the body of Christ, and members in particular." Here he identified them. Then he defined what he meant by "the Church," emphasizing again the oneness that the Lord requires:

"And God hath set some in the church, first apostles, secondarily prophets, thirdly teachers, after that miracles, then gifts of healings, helps, governments, diversities of tongues.

"Are all apostles? are all prophets? are all teachers? are all workers of miracles?

"Have all the gifts of healing? do all speak with tongues? do all interpret?" (1 Corinthians 12:27-30.)

He wrote similarly to the Ephesians when he described the Church:

"And he gave some, apostles; and some, prophets; and some, evangelists; and some, pastors and teachers;

"For the perfecting of the saints, for the work of the ministry, for the edifying of the body of Christ:

"Till we all come in the unity of the faith, and of the knowledge of the Son of God, unto a perfect man, unto the measure of the stature of the fulness of Christ:

"That we henceforth be no more children, tossed to and fro, and carried about with every wind of doctrine, by the sleight of men, and cunning craftiness, whereby they lie in wait to deceive;

"But speaking the truth in love, may grow up into him in all things, which is the head, even Christ:

"From whom the whole body fitly joined together and compacted by that which every joint supplieth, according to the effectual working in the measure of every part, maketh increase of the body unto the edifying of itself in love." (Ephesians 4:11-16.)

Note particularly that he said, "That we henceforth be no more children, tossed to and fro, and carried about with every wind of doctrine, by the sleight of men, and cunning craftiness, whereby they lie in wait to deceive." This was to preserve that oneness.

But in spite of all these efforts to teach unity, divisions appeared, nevertheless, just opposite to what the Lord commanded.

A schism occurred among the Corinthians to whom Paul had sent an epistle. In fact, it was because of that rupture that he wrote his appeal.

He charged them with falling away from the faith. They no longer believed in the resurrection of the Lord. This caused him to write his brilliant defense of that doctrine. (1 Corinthians 15.)

He accused them of breaking up into four factions, one following Paul, one Apollos, one Cephas (Peter), and another that called itself after Christ.

And then he demanded: *"Is Christ divided?"* (1 Corinthians 1:13. Italics added.)

To emphasize his treatise on unity, he said:

"Now I beseech you, brethren, by the name of our Lord Jesus Christ, that ye all speak the same thing, and that there be no divisions among you; but that ye be perfectly joined together in the same mind and in the same judgment." (1 Corinthians 1:10.)

The Savior knew that many would fall away from the truth. He made this very clear as He foretold apostate conditions which would arise after His death and also those which would precede His second coming. (Matthew 24:10-13, 24.)

Apostasy occurred among the Jews even before the Savior was born. He had to contend with it throughout His adult life. Departure from the Law of Moses resulted in the formation of several different denominations and persuasions. This was so pronounced in Jesus' day that He said to the Jews:

"Did not Moses give you the law, and yet none of you keepeth the law?" (John 7:19.)

What different denominations of Jewry were there in His day?

There were:

1. Pharisees, who re-wrote much of the law to suit their own liking.

2. Sadducees and Zadokites, who denied the resurrection.

3. Essenes, who rejected temple worship and lived in celibacy.

4. Zealots, an anti-Roman cult.

5. Hellenists, who had accepted Greek inroads into the law of Moses and rejected temple worship.

6. Herodians sponsored by Herod.

Much foreign influence had resulted from the Greek and Roman political dominance of Palestine arising out of the conquest by Alexander the Great and the infusion of Greek settlers there.

The first great falling away among the followers of Jesus came almost as soon as He began to preach. His pure doctrine was in stark contrast to the erroneous teachings which had been imposed upon the people and they would not accept it. The reaction saddened the Savior.

"From that time many of his disciples went back, and walked no more with him.

"Then said Jesus unto the twelve, Will ye also go away?

"Then Simon Peter answered him, Lord, to whom shall we go? thou hast the words of eternal life.

"And we believe and are sure that thou art that Christ, the Son of the living God." (John 6:66-69.)

Divisions and apostasies produced man-made creeds then as now. The Savior recognized this, of course, and spoke strongly against them, saying there is no salvation in them at all!

"In vain do they worship me, teaching for doctrines the commandments of men." (Matthew 15:9.)

Or as the Roman Catholic Jerusalem Bible expresses it in Mark 7:6-9:

"This people honors me only with lip service, while their hearts are far from me. *The worship they offer me is worthless.* The doctrines they teach are only human regulations." (Italics added.)

Then can there be a diversity of Christian churches and all of them be true? Did He organize more than one? Can discordant creeds bring salvation? Is there conflict in Christ?

Does religious freedom include the right to alter the sacred teachings of the Savior? Can people decide for themselves how they will conduct Christian worship?

With Him there is but one way—His way—for He is the Good Shepherd, and He tells us that there is only one door and one sheepfold.

And again, what is that sheepfold? It is His Church. But which of the many sects is His? There are hundreds to choose from and they have a wide variety of creeds, all supposedly expounding true Christian doctrine. But do they? Can they, when they are in conflict one with another? Which is right?

Or will any one of them suffice, just any one, with the thought that "all roads lead to Rome"?

Is the truth limited to but one church? If so, is that one true church really on the earth today? Are there some definite marks of identification by which we may recognize this church?

His own Church—His own sheepfold—is now on the earth in unmistakable certainty. These marks of identification are obvious for all to see, just as they were in the time of Peter and Paul. Let us note what they are, that we may truly learn which church is right.

Jesus is the door today as He was anciently. He never changes. He calls to each of us now—as He did anciently—and says, "By me, if any man enter in, he shall be saved." (John 10:9.)

But, He says—it must be "by me."

Chapter Two

Clear Identification

There can be no uncertainty about the existence of the Church of Jesus Christ in ancient times. He did have a church, and He organized it with twelve apostles and prophets as its foundation. He also introduced specific doctrines and ordinances, many of which have been altered or ignored.

Can we forget His words spoken to those very apostles, when He declared, "upon this rock I will build my church"? (Matthew 16:18.)

The scores of references to His Church as they appear in Acts, the Epistles, and in the book of Revelation should convince even the most skeptical. He did have a church.

When passages are read such as "the churches of Christ salute you" (Romans 16:16), it is not to be supposed that Jesus organized more than one institution. Such references relate to branches of the one Church, whether in Palestine, Asia, Italy, or Greece.

There was but one true Church, with branches in various cities, and they were all supervised by that one group of General Authorities, the twelve Apostles. This made them all "one Church."

The twelve formed the foundation of the Church, with Christ as the chief cornerstone, "in whom all the building fitly framed together groweth unto an holy temple in the Lord: In whom ye also are builded together for an habitation of God through the Spirit." (Ephesians 2:19-22.)

So there was but one building "fitly framed together," although comprised of many branches united in one "holy temple in the Lord," and one "habitation of God through the Spirit."

So the Lord did not organize a variety of denominations. He had but one, and it was not to be subdivided.

The Church as the Lord provided it had a definite list of doctrines to which its members subscribed. It had its own plan of organization differing from that set forth in the law of Moses to which the Jews were accustomed.

His Church had specific ordinances not subject to change or cancellation. The members, too, were known by their own particular name. They were not Pharisees, nor Sadducees, nor Herodians, nor Essenes. They were the Saints of God.

Current revelation was an integral part of that Church, with prophets and revelators who received those revelations. How could God guide His Church if He did not communicate with it? Were not these communications actually revelations? And who could receive revelations for the Church but the prophets?

It was Amos who said that the Lord God will do nothing but through His prophets, and certainly it was through them that He directed His people anciently. (Amos 3:7.) Has He changed His ways today?

Divine authority was an all-important part of His Church. Persons not called by current revelation given through living prophets were not chosen by Him. It was that simple, for "no man taketh this honour unto himself, but he that is called of God, as was Aaron." (Hebrews 5:4.)

How was Aaron called? By current revelation through a living prophet. (Exodus 28:1-4.) That was the pattern. No exceptions were made.

The creeds of men brought in sad changes in doctrine. For example, some taught that unbaptized children were lost. But the Savior said little children were of the kingdom of heaven. They were not consigned to any place of darkness and pain if they died without being christened, as some claimed; neither were they cast aside for any other reason. They are of "the kingdom of heaven." (Matthew 19:14.)

And the hosts of the dead—what of them? Can the dead be saved, even those who lived and died before the Savior came into the world? Of course they can, and in the same way everyone else will receive that blessing. And by what means? The gospel is for all mankind, living and dead, regardless of when they lived in mortality or where. He Himself taught that He is the God of both the living and the dead, for all live unto Him. (Luke 20:38.)

Did not Jesus visit the dead and preach to them, and was not that to help them live "according to God in the spirit"? (1 Peter 3:18-20; 4:6.)

The gospel was not alone for the Jews, either. It was for all the world, every nation, kindred, tongue, and people. (Matthew 28:19-20.) But it was the twelve apostles who were commanded to preach it that broadly. Is not that one of the signs of the true Church—that the worldwide preaching of the gospel would be directed by the twelve apostles? Who else could do it? Who else had been commissioned? Who else had the divine authority to do so? (Mark 16:15.)

Important to His Church was a correct understanding of what God is like, that man is created in His image. Idolatry was rampant in that day and had been for ages. The true knowledge of God was possessed by such men as Moses, who actually saw Him and talked with Him face to face. It was also known to Peter and Paul and the disciples of their day. But most people did not comprehend.

As apostasy came into the world the true knowledge of God disappeared even from among those who claimed to be Christians. How can anyone really worship a Being if they do not know what he is like? Of what value is an unknown Deity?

God was revealed in that day through the personal and mortal life of the Savior. "He that hath seen me, hath seen the Father" He told His disciples, illustrating that indeed He was in the image of the "invisible God." (John 14:9; Colossians 1:15.)

The Church revealed the truth about the origin of the earth, also, and of life itself, another mark of identification. All things came by divine creation, and Christ was the Creator. This knowledge is fundamental to Christianity. (John 1:1-5; Colossians 1:14-17.)

Immortality and the Resurrection—these vital factors of the gospel of Christ—what of them? Christ demonstrated that both are of Him, and His true disciples accepted those truths. But in the "falling away" they were denied. (1 Corinthians 15.)

As the Creator, Jesus lived in a premortal existence, but so did we. And He lived after His death. So will we! As the Savior, He broke the bands of death. Remember that He said: "I am the resurrection, and the life." And was it not so? (John 11:25.)

The true Church was a well-organized institution with clearly defined teachings and practices. However, it was lost to mankind. Apostasy took over, and drove the truth away.

But now it has returned, the Church with all its divine gifts and blessings. Salvation is again available to mankind through the true sheepfold of Christ, and He is the door.

Did He not say: "By me, if any man enter in, he shall be saved"? (John 10:9.)

But "by me"!

Chapter Three

The Body and Its Parts

The true Church of Jesus Christ has many unmistakable marks of identification. They are essential parts of the "body of Christ." All must be present to complete the identification. Just a few will not do.

As Paul expressed it so clearly, "the body is not one member, but many. If the foot shall say, Because I am not the hand, I am not of the body; is it therefore not of the body?

"And if the ear shall say, Because I am not the eye, I am not of the body; is it therefore not of the body?

"If the whole body were an eye, where were the hearing? If the whole were hearing, where were the smelling?

"But now hath God set the members every one of them in the body, as it hath pleased him. And if they were all one member, where were the body? But now are they many members, yet one body.

"And the eye cannot say unto the hand, I have no need of thee: nor again the head to the feet, I have no need of you." (1 Corinthians 12:14-21.)

Any given sect may have one or two marks of the true Church, but it still would not be the Church for the whole must be there. The body must be perfect, not lacking any essential part. And all parts must be "fitly joined together." There is nothing haphazard with the Lord.

In his dissertation, Paul explained some of the characteristics of the Church, and referred among other things to its spiritual gifts. But he quickly added that the Church consists not only of spiritual gifts, or "where were the Church?"

He went on to say:

"Now there are diversities of gifts, but the same Spirit.

"And there are differences of administrations, but the same Lord.

"And there are diversities of operations, but it is the same God which worketh all in all.

"But the manifestation of the Spirit is given to every man to profit withal.

"For to one is given by the Spirit the word of wisdom; to another the word of knowledge by the same Spirit;

"To another faith by the same Spirit; to another the gifts of healing by the same Spirit;

"To another the working of miracles; to another prophecy; to another discerning of spirits; to another divers kinds of tongues; to another the interpretation of tongues:

"But all these worketh that one and the selfsame Spirit, dividing to every man severally as he will.

"For as the body is one, and hath many members, and all the members of that one body, being many, are one body: so also is Christ.

"For by one Spirit are we all baptized into one body, whether we be Jews or Gentiles, whether we be bond or free; and have been all made to drink into one Spirit.

"For the body is not one member, but many." (1 Corinthians 12:4-14.)

Then he said:

"Now ye are the body of Christ, and members in particular." (1 Corinthians 12:27.) Thus he designated his converts. Indeed they were members of the Church of Jesus Christ. They belonged to His "body," but they were unmistakably told that there were many parts to the body, and that all are required. Otherwise, "where were the body?"

And then Paul pointed out some of the fundamental facets of the Church in addition to the spiritual gifts previously mentioned:

"And God hath set some in the church, first apostles, secondarily prophets, thirdly teachers, after that miracles, then gifts of healings, helps, governments, diversities of tongues.

"Are all apostles? are all prophets? are all teachers? are all workers of miracles?

"Have all the gifts of healing? do all speak with tongues? do all interpret?" (1 Corinthians 12:28-30.)

So, a specific organization of officials characterized the Church and formed one of the great marks of its identification. Furthermore, he says that the organization was headed by "first apostles, secondarily prophets."

Why would he thus mention them?

In his epistle to the Ephesians, he explained that the apostles and prophets are the *foundation* of the Church, (Ephesians 2:20-22) and here again he mentioned that the parts must be fitly joined together.

But he goes even further in this passage and says that in those apostles and prophets and in Jesus Christ who is the chief cornerstone of the entire structure—or as one version says *by* this group—is "all the building fitly framed together" and "groweth unto an holy temple in the Lord."

Examine those words. If the apostles and prophets are the foundation of the Church, what would happen if they were removed? What would happen to any building if the foundation was removed?

And what if Christ—the chief cornerstone—is removed, as He effectually has been from some denominations that refuse to regard Him as the divine Son of God? Some openly reject His resurrection and abolish His command to be baptized.

Would there be a true Church of Christ if the basic teachings of Christ were removed? Would that not constitute a removal of Christ Himself?

He is the chief cornerstone. Is not the cornerstone a part of the foundation? Must we not consider the foundation and the cornerstone as integral parts of the structure of any building? And must we not also consider Christ and His Twelve as an indivisible group? Can we take either one out of the Church and think it is still the Church?

As a house would collapse without its foundation, so would—and did—the early Church of Jesus Christ.

When either Christ or His apostles, or both, are absent, where in fact is the Church?

Without the apostles (who are notably absent from worldly churches), is the eye saying to the hand, "I have no need of thee?" Or is the head saying to the feet, "I have no need of thee?"

But the apostles and prophets are the head of the Church! Can the feet say to the head, or an elder or a bishop say to an apostle or prophet, "I have no need of thee?" And if they did, "where were the Church?"

No church, lacking living apostles and prophets, truly inspired of the Lord by current revelation, can lay even a remote claim to being the true Church of Jesus Christ, else, again as Paul said, "Where were the body?" Indeed as Paul told the Ephesians, all parts of the body must be there, fitly joined together. And as he told them further:

"I therefore, the prisoner of the Lord, beseech you that ye walk worthy of the vocation wherewith ye are called,

"With all lowliness and meekness, with longsuffering, forbearing one another in love;

"Endeavouring to keep the unity of the Spirit in the bond of peace.

"There is one body, and one Spirit, even as ye are called in one hope of your calling;

"One Lord, one faith (only one true gospel), one baptism,

"One God and Father of all, who is above all, and through all, and in you all." (Ephesians 4:1-6.)

Then can there possibly be more than one organization of true Christianity?

Certain Christian clerics claim that the numerous denominations of Christianity make up the body of Christ, conflicting though they be.

But they teach different doctrines. There is nothing harmonious about them. There is no unity among them. They openly oppose each other.

Certainly they are not of one mind. They are not "perfectly joined together" as Paul said.

They may claim to be parts of a worldwide Christianity, but they are a splintered Christianity, broken up into conflicting denominations. There is no such division in Christ.

Chapter Four

The Foundation Stone

As the Apostle Paul described the ancient Church, he wrote: "Jesus Christ himself being the chief corner stone." (Ephesians 2:20.)

And so He is. The chief cornerstone of the Lord's true Church is the Savior Himself, and none other. The other foundation stones were the apostles and prophets, but the chief cornerstone was *Christ.*

All Christian denominations claim to be churches of Christ, saying they teach His gospel as the way to salvation. But when they say they believe in Christ, what do they mean? And do they all understand alike?

The Savior warned against false Christs (Matthew 24). Do man-made creeds foster a false Christianity by their erroneous teachings?

As it drifted from the truth, the early Church was ruptured by a debate over the nature of God. Prominent in those disputations was a man named Arius who later opposed Athanasius in the Council of Nicea. He denied the godhood of the Savior, although admitting that He was the Son of God, but not possessing the powers of divinity.

He was excommunicated twice from the early Church as it was erroneously constituted in his day. The first time was in A.D. 311 when he was known as a deacon. His schismatic views in reality were borrowed from Meletius, a fourth century bishop at Lycopolis. Arius was reinstated in A.D. 313 and was made a presbyter at Baucalus.

There he came into great prominence by teaching that Christ was created by God, that He was less than God but a little above men. He popularized his views with widespread publications, for which he was firmly censured in A.D. 318, but he still persisted in his rebellion.

A "patriarch" of that church, whose name was Alexander, convened a synod of bishops and excommunicated Arius in A.D. 321 for the second time.

The well-known Eusebius, bishop of Nicodemia, endorsed Arius and his work, causing a wide split in the Church, finally resulting in the call of the Nicene Council by Constantine the Great in A.D. 325.

After weeks of debate between Arius and his supporters and Athanasius and his, the Council anathematized and banished Arius.

The ardent rebel would not give up. He went to Constantine personally and converted him. It is to be admitted that the emperor was a pagan, although he was the primary influence in the Nicene Council, and strongly supported Athanasius there. It was this support which had led to the banishment of Arius.

But when Constantine now heard Arius, he was sympathetic. Doctrine really meant nothing to this pagan ruler, but persuasion did. Being convinced by Arius, the emperor now commanded Athanasius to admit Arius to communion. When Athanasius refused, the synod of Tyre (A.D. 335) exiled him to Gaul.

Constantine at this point commanded the bishop of Constantinople to restore Arius to communion. However, Arius died on the day of the ceremony.

But the seeds planted by Arius never withered away. They continue to sprout, and even today widely accepted denominations carry his torch and hold that Jesus is not divine.

One of those churches, in its own translation of the Bible, renders John 1:1 as follows:

"In the beginning was the Word and the Word was with God, and the word was a god." They refuse to capitalize the "g" in this scripture, thus supporting their erroneous conclusion. (New World Translation.) Theirs is the only translation that does this. They did capitalize the "W" in "the Word," but why is not explained, since their capitalized "Word" refers to the same Being to whom they denied capitalization in the word "god."

Other denominations today refuse to believe in His resurrection. For what it may be worth, a survey was taken by Jeffrey Hadden, a Western Reserve University sociologist, and published in *Christianity Today* on October 13, 1967. Hadden claimed to have contacted 10,000 clergymen in the United States. Of that number, 7,441 replied.

These ministers were asked if they believed in a physical resurrection. More than a third said no. More than half claimed they did not believe in the virgin birth of Christ. When asked if they believe in a personal devil, the same number said no. When asked if the Bible was an inspired book to be accepted literally as the word of God, in one denomination 89 percent said no, in another 82 percent, in still another 81, and others ranged down to a figure of 57 percent negative. (*Christian Crusade,* Tulsa, Oklahoma.)

With respect to the resurrection, several of the best-known denominations teach that at death, both body and spirit go into the grave, remaining there lifeless ("for the dead knoweth nothing"). Then on resurrection day, they say only the spirit comes forth, not the body. They deny any physical resurrection.

All of this enters into a definition of Christ. What Christ do they worship? The true Christ, or some false Christ in the form of a demi-god? The ancient Greeks believed in demi-gods, men who were the supposed offspring of mortal women with whom the gods of Mount Olympus cohabitated. But it was all mythology. Are the false Christs of today in the same category?

Many non-Christians now admit that Jesus of Nazareth was a great teacher, even a leading rabbi, but they refuse to accept Him as the Son of God. They deny His divinity. To them He was merely a great teacher, in the same category as Confucius or Mohammed.

His claim to being the Son of God is what precipitated His crucifixion. But deny Him as His crucifiers did, can their false deductions change the facts in the matter? Can denials of modern denominations rob Him of His divine status? Truly the "wisdom" of man is foolishness to God.

The definition of God in the minds of most Christians is, of course, set forth in the creeds of their various denominations. Most of them reflect the views of Athanasius as set forth at the Nicene Council, but altered from time to time as subsequent synods of the fourth, fifth, and sixth centuries changed their minds.

The extent of the split in the Church of that day, as they debated the nature of God, is evident in the fact that after Arius was restored to communion, more than a hundred bishops openly advocated his view.

Athanasius was brought back from exile following the death of Constantine. Pope Julius declared him innocent and sustained his views on the nature of Deity.

At this time 300 bishops assembled at Sardica and confirmed their belief in the Athanasian creed, but at the same time a hundred other bishops met in Alexandria, and declared their belief in the Arian creed.

Out of his forty-six years in public life, Athanasius spent twenty years in banishment as the apostate church vacillated from one side to the other, depending on its leadership, some of the time accepting the Arian creed—denying the divinity of Christ—and part of the time sustaining the Athanasian creed, which made Christ "of one substance" with the Father.

As the creeds were rewritten from time to time in those years, changes finally brought about what is known as the Apostles' Creed, so named to give it the appearance of authenticity. It forms the basis of the liturgies of most of the established denominations of today.

For the most part, they still accept such expressions with respect to Deity as:

"We worship one God in trinity and trinity in unity, neither confounding the persons nor dividing the substance. . . . there are not three Incomprehensibles but one Incomprehensible . . . so the Father is God, the Son is God and the Holy Ghost is God; yet they are not three Gods but one God. So the Father is Lord, the Son is Lord, and the Holy Ghost is Lord, and yet not three Lords but one Lord, . . . they are not three Almighties, but one Almighty. . . . For like as we are compelled by Christian verity to acknowledge every person by himself to be God and Lord, so are we forbidden to say there be three Gods or three Lords."

Typical excerpts from the creeds of today, defining the nature of God, read that He is:

"An infinite spirit without form or body, everywhere present."

"An invisible spiritual substance everywhere present at once."

"An infinite spirit everywhere present at the same time, without form, body, parts or passions."

"A spirit without body, parts or passions, of incomprehensible shape, everywhere present at once."

"There is no form or shape connected with God; He is a Spirit without body, parts or passions."

"He is Universal Intelligence, everywhere present at once, without form, or body or shape."

To show how erroneous doctrines crept into the true Church, we have this from the *Twentieth Century Encyclopedia of Catholicism* (vol. 17, pp. 117-137):

"What would have happened if St. Athanasius had not made use of Greek thought as well as scripture? . . . From the religious point of view Christianity could never have over-ridden the differences between Greek and Barbarian, Jew and Gentile, if it had remained Jewish in its way of thought, if it had not acquired through contact with the Greek genius, that suppleness which enabled it to reach all systems of thought." (p. 118.)

On page 123 of this same encyclopedia we read:

"Greek theology was well adapted to become a marvelous guide to express for man the depth of his relationship with God."

Comments on the Holy Spirit, as provided in this volume, are of interest in showing the extent of the departure from the truth which developed in those days.

"St. Augustine departed from the Greek exposition of the subject. Augustine showed that the Holy Spirit proceeds from the Father and the Son—that the Father and Son are entranced with love for each other, that they meet in love which is common to them both, *and that love is the Holy Spirit.*" (p. 124, italics added.)

And then this appears:

"This love is the Holy Spirit of whom St. Bernard said that He is the kiss exchanged between Father and Son." (p. 131.)

In Saint Augustine's book, *The City of God,* the author teaches that the breath of God is the Holy Ghost, and it was this breath which He breathed into Adam to make him live. (See pages 438-440.)

Thus the so-called Christian world lost sight of the Being whom they professed to worship.

But who and what is the true Christ in literal reality? Let us examine the facts, for no church can claim to be His if it rejects His basic doctrines. Such rejection automatically eliminates a number of the claimants.

Chapter Five

His Preexistent Divinity

Jesus of Nazareth—who is He?

The real Christ is the beloved and Only Begotten Son of God. He was that Mighty Being who volunteered to become our Savior during the Primeval Council in Heaven.

He it was who said in our First Estate: "Father, thy will be done, and the glory be thine forever." (Moses 4:2.)

It was that same Being, Jesus of Nazareth, who in Gethsemane as the Lamb of God about to be slain for the sins of the world, expressed Himself in those same sublime terms: "Not my will, but thine, be done." (Luke 22:42.)

Abraham had been shown the Savior in a vision of the great spirits of the preexistence. He said:

"Now the Lord had shown unto me, Abraham, the intelligences that were organized before the world was; and among all these there were many of the noble and great ones;

"And God saw these souls that they were good, and he stood in the midst of them, and he said: These I will make my rulers; for he stood among those that were spirits, and he saw that they were good; and he said unto me: Abraham, thou art one of them; thou wast chosen before thou wast born." (Abraham 3:22-23.)

Then Abraham was shown "One among them that was like unto God and he said unto those who were with him:

"We will go down, for there is space there, and we will take of these materials, and we will make an earth whereon these may dwell;

"And we will prove them herewith, to see if they will do all things whatsoever the Lord their God shall command them;

"And they who keep their first estate shall be added upon; and they who keep not their first estate shall not have glory in the same kingdom with those who keep their first estate; and they who keep their second estate shall have glory added upon their heads for ever and ever.

"And the Lord said: Whom shall I send? And one answered like unto the Son of Man: Here am I, send me. And another answered and said: Here am I, send me. And the Lord said: I will send the first.

"And the second was angry, and kept not his first estate; and at that day, many followed after him." (Abraham 3:24-28.)

The angry one became Lucifer, the devil, who rebelled against God, having sought His glory. As Moses wrote of that primeval council, describing the rebellion of Lucifer, he said:

"And I, the Lord God, spake unto Moses, saying: That Satan, whom thou hast commanded in the name of mine Only Begotten, is the same which was from the beginning, and he came before me saying—Behold, here am I, send me, I will be thy son, and I will redeem all mankind, that one soul shall not be lost, and surely I will do it; wherefore give me thine honor.

"But, behold, my Beloved Son, which was my Beloved and Chosen from the beginning, said unto me—Father, thy will be done, and the glory be thine forever.

"Wherefore, because that Satan rebelled against me, and sought to destroy the agency of man, which I, the Lord God, had given him, and also, that I should give unto him mine own power; by the power of mine Only Begotten, I caused that he should be cast down;

"And he became Satan, yea, even the devil, the father of all lies, to deceive and to blind men, and to lead them captive at his will, even as many as would not hearken unto my voice." (Moses 4:1-4.)

The Lord revealed this rebellion to the Prophet Joseph Smith of which he wrote:

"And this we saw also, and bear record, that an angel of God who was in authority in the presence of God, who rebelled against the Only Begotten Son whom the Father loved and who was in the bosom of the Father, was thrust down from the presence of God and the Son,

"And was called Perdition, for the heavens wept over him—he was Lucifer, a son of the morning.

"And we beheld, and lo, he is fallen! is fallen, even a son of the morning!

"And while we were yet in the Spirit, the Lord commanded us that we should write the vision; for we beheld Satan, that old serpent, even the devil, who rebelled against God, and sought to take the kingdom of our God and his Christ—

"Wherefore, he maketh war with the saints of God, and encompasseth them round about." (D & C 76:25-29.)

So there is a devil, and he does fight against God and the Saints.

But of the Savior, Jesus Christ, Joseph Smith wrote:

"And we beheld the glory of the Son, on the right hand of the Father, and received of his fulness;

"And saw the holy angels, and them who are sanctified before his throne, worshiping God, and the Lamb, who worship him forever and ever.

"And now, after the many testimonies which have been given of him, this is the testimony, last of all, which we give of him: That he lives!

"For we saw him, even on the right hand of God; and we heard the voice bearing record that he is the Only Begotten of the Father—

"That by him, and through him, and of him, the worlds are and were created, and the inhabitants thereof are begotten sons and daughters unto God." (D & C 76:20-24.)

That is the identification of Jesus Christ. He was the Firstborn of the Father in the preexistence and the Only Begotten in the flesh; He was on the right hand of God. He was the Creator of all the worlds.

Christ attained Godhood in His preexistence, long before His birth into mortality. As Deity in heaven—together with His Eternal Father and ours—He became the Creator of all the universes, all the worlds, all the galaxies, all the earths, and He gave life to all living things.

That is the real Christ.

As John said, "All things were made by him; and without him was not any thing made that was made." (John 1:3.)

Paul described Him in this way:

"In whom we have redemption through his blood, even the forgiveness of sins:

"Who is the image of the invisible God, the firstborn of every creature:

"For by him were all things created, that are in heaven, and that are in earth, visible and invisible, whether they be thrones, or dominions, or principalities, or powers: all things were created by him, and for him:

"And he is before all things, and by him all things consist.

"And he is the head of the body, the church: who is the beginning, the firstborn from the dead; that in all things he might have the preeminence.

"For it pleased the Father that in him should all fulness dwell;

"And, having made peace through the blood of his cross, by him to reconcile all things unto himself; by him, I say, whether they be things in earth, or things in heaven." (Colossians 1:14-20.)

Concerning the Creator we have this from the writings of Moses:

"Worlds without number have I created; and I also created them for mine own purpose; and by the Son I created them, which is mine Only Begotten." (Moses 1:33.)

As Enoch described His creations he said:

"And were it possible that man could number the particles of the earth, yea, millions of earths like this, it would not be a beginning to the number of thy creations; and thy curtains are stretched out still; and yet thou art there, and thy bosom is there; and also thou art just; thou art merciful and kind forever." (Moses 7:30.)

When Paul wrote to the Hebrews, he taught:

"God, who at sundry times and in divers manners spake in time past unto the fathers by the prophets,

"Hath in these last days spoken unto us by his Son, whom he hath appointed heir of all things, by whom also he made the worlds;

"Who being the brightness of his glory, and the express image of his person, and upholding all things by the word of his power, when he had by himself purged our sins, sat down on the right hand of the Majesty on high." (Hebrews 1:1-3.)

Other Bible translations of John 1:1-4 confirm these statements:

Barclay (Church of Scotland): "He was the agent through whom all things were made and there was not a single thing which exists in this world which came into being without Him."

Goodspeed: "Everything came into existence through Him and apart from Him nothing came to be."

Knox (Catholic): "It was through Him that all things came into being, and without Him came nothing that has come to be."

New English: "Through Him all things came to be; no single thing was created without Him."

New World: "All things came into existence through Him, and apart from Him not even one thing came into existence."

"Schoenfeld: "By Him everything had being."

Jerusalem (Catholic): "Through Him all things came to be. Not one thing had its beginning but through Him."

It is heartwarming to read what He himself said as He gave revelations to the Prophet Joseph Smith:

"Listen to the voice of the Lord your God, even Alpha and Omega, the beginning and the end, whose course is one eternal round, the same today as yesterday, and forever.

"I am Jesus Christ, the Son of God, who was crucified for the sins of the world, even as many as will believe on my name, that they may become the sons of God, even one in me as I am one in the Father, as the Father is one in me, that we may be one." (D & C 35:1-2.)

And then He said this about Himself:

"Hearken, O ye people of my church, to whom the kingdom has been given; hearken ye and give ear to him who laid the foundation of the earth, who made the heavens and all the hosts thereof, and by whom all things were made which live, and move, and have a being.

"And again I say, hearken unto my voice, lest death shall overtake you; in an hour when ye think not the summer shall be past, and the harvest ended, and your souls not saved.

"Listen to him who is the advocate with the Father, who is pleading your cause before him—

"Saying: Father, behold the sufferings and death of him who did no sin, in whom thou wast well pleased; behold the blood of thy Son which was shed, the blood of him whom thou gavest that thyself might be glorified;

"Wherefore, Father, spare these my brethren that believe on my name, that they may come unto me and have everlasting life.

"Hearken, O ye people of my church, and ye elders listen together, and hear my voice while it is called today, and harden not your hearts;

"For verily I say unto you that I am Alpha and Omega, the beginning and the end, the light and the life of the world—a light that shineth in darkness and the darkness comprehendeth it not.

"I came unto mine own, and mine own received me not; but unto as many as received me gave I power to do many miracles, and to become the sons of God; and even unto them that believed on my name gave I power to obtain eternal life.

"And even so I have sent mine everlasting covenant into the world, to be a light to the world, and to be a standard for my people, and for the Gentiles to seek to it, and to be a messenger before my face to prepare the way before me." (D & C 45:1-9.)

Only a divine Being could create all things. Christ was the Creator. And He is divine.

This is borne out in some of the newer translations of the first chapter of John. Says the Goodspeed American translation: "In the beginning the Word existed. The Word was with God, and the Word was divine."

Schoenfeld's Authentic New Testament: "In the beginning was the Word, and the Word was with God, so the Word was divine."

The New English Bible says it slightly differently, but with the same meaning: "When all things began, the Word already was. The Word dwelt with God, and what God was, the Word was." Christ was divine.

The Knox (Catholic) version: "At the beginning of time the Word already was. And God had the Word abiding with Him, and the Word was God."

Not only do these passages verify the divinity of Christ, and sustain the fact of His being the Creator, but they also teach that the Father and the Son are two separate Beings, as are any father and son, "and what the Father was, the Word was."

When the time came for Jesus to be born on earth, His divinity was declared once again. It will be remembered that Isaiah predicted His birth, and that His mother would be a virgin. In that prediction Isaiah identified Jesus as being divine—as being God.

Matthew quoted Isaiah telling of Jesus' birth, and wrote:

"Behold, a virgin shall be with child, and shall bring forth a son, and they shall call his name Emmanuel, which being interpreted is, *God with us.*" (Matthew 1:23. Italics added.) For whom else would the angels sing? They sang hosannahs to Him at His birth. They knew His true identity.

Throughout his ministry, as recorded in the New Testament, He testified of Himself as the Son of God—the Redeemer, the Messiah—and He testified also of His Eternal Father, whom He constantly honored.

One of the most touching instances of this kind transpired as Jesus sat with the Samaritan woman at the well, and she spoke of the expected Messiah. The humble Savior, Creator of all things, but now a traveling preacher in Palestine, said to her: "I that speak unto thee am He." (John 4:26.)

In the midst of His passion, as He suffered so deeply, "the high priest asked him, and said unto him, Art thou the Christ, the Son of the Blessed? And Jesus said, I am." (Mark 14:61-62.)

His appearance to the Book of Mormon people provided further identification. As He descended from heaven, following His resurrection, He testified:

"Behold, I am Jesus Christ, whom the prophets testified shall come into the world.

"And behold, I am the light and the life of the world; and I have drunk out of that bitter cup which the Father hath given me, and have glorified the Father in taking upon me the sins of the world, in the which I have suffered the will of the Father in all things from the beginning." (3 Nephi 11:10-11.)

When He appeared in the Kirtland Temple, He spoke to Joseph Smith and Oliver Cowdery:

"The veil was taken from our minds, and the eyes of our understanding were opened.

"We saw the Lord standing upon the breastwork of the pulpit, before us; and under his feet was a paved work of pure gold, in color like amber.

"His eyes were as a flame of fire; the hair of his head was white like the pure snow; his countenance shone above the brightness of the sun; and his voice was as the sound of the rushing of great waters, even the voice of Jehovah, saying:

"I am the first and the last; I am he who liveth, I am he was was slain; I am your advocate with the Father." (D & C 110:1-4.)

Then who is Christ? The divine Son of God, our Savior and Redeemer, our Creater — the long-expected Messiah.

Conversion to Him would be incomplete without acceptance of His resurrection. It was a real, flesh and bone resurrection. His body still bore the marks of the Crucifixion as proof of His corporeal reality.

"Handle me, and see," He declared to His apostles, "for a spirit hath not flesh and bones, as ye see me have." (Luke 24:39.)

He ate with His disciples, again demonstrating the fact of His flesh and bone resurrection.

He was real. He was Christ. He was divine, and acceptance of Him in this manner must be one of the signs of the true Church.

The Father's recognition of His Son is the most impressive of all declarations concerning the Savior. The Father identified and acknowledged Him unreservedly. Repeatedly He declared: "This is My Beloved Son in whom I am well pleased. Hear ye Him." And that is a command!

If we believe in the Father, can we doubt His Son? God was well pleased with the divine Savior. Should we not be pleased with Him, too?

Then we must measure our recognition of Christ's Church in part by a proper identification which He gives of Himself:

He was the First Born of God in the Spirit, the Only Begotten in the flesh.

He was the Creator of heaven and earth and all life.

He was the Babe of Bethlehem, Emmanual, "God with us."

He died on the cross for the sins of all mankind.

He brought about the resurrection of the dead.

He was divine, being a member of the heavenly Trinity of three personal but separate Gods in one Godhead.

He is the Savior of the Christians, the Messiah of the Jews.

This identification of Christ, then, becomes the major mark by which we will recognize His Church.

But even this acceptance is not enough to fully identify any given denomination as His own. The true Church must have all of its parts, fitly joined together. Important as is the identification of Christ, it is but one of the many true marks by which we may recognize the Lord's true Church.

Chapter Six

There Is a Trinity

One of the great signs of the true Church is the correct doctrine of God, the Godhead, and the literal Fatherhood of God.

There are three in the Trinity—Father, Son and Holy Ghost.

"The Father has a body of flesh and bones as tangible as man's; the Son also; but the Holy Ghost has not a body of flesh and bones, but is a personage of Spirit. Were it not so, the Holy Ghost could not dwell in us." (D & C 130:22.)

The Father indeed is the literal Father of us all. We did not spring from lower forms of life. We are the offspring—the children —of Deity. The Father of Jesus Christ is our Father also, in the spirit. We lived with Him in our pre-earth life. We were living persons then as we are now. We could be identified then as such, even as now. We never change our identity.

When the Greeks on Mars' Hill were worshipping an "unknown God," Paul preached the true doctrine of Deity to them. After describing Him in reality, as not being made of wood or stone, he said:

"For in him we live, and move, and have our being; as certain also of your own poets have said, For we are also his offspring.

"Forasmuch then as we are the offspring of God, we ought not to think that the Godhead is like unto gold, or silver, or stone, graven by art and man's device." (Acts 17:28-29.)

He pursued the thought still further to the Hebrews as he wrote:

"Furthermore we have had fathers of our flesh which corrected us, and we gave them reverence: shall we not much rather be in subjection unto the Father of spirits, and live?" (Hebrews 12:9.)

Why would Jesus teach us to pray to our Father in heaven if God is not our Father? (Matthew 6:9.) Why would He teach us the doctrine of forgiveness of sins—from our Heavenly Father? (Matthew 6:14-15.) Why would He say to Mary, following the Resurrection:

"Touch me not; for I am not yet ascended to my Father: but go to my brethren, and say unto them, I ascend unto my Father, and your Father; and to my God, and your God." (John 20:17.)

The full acceptance of God as our Father is one of the primary doctrines and marks of identification of the true Church.

To properly understand the Fatherhood of God, we must know the reason for our existence here on earth. The divine purpose with respect to ourselves is that we become like Him. Is it not natural for a mortal son to become like his mortal father? The principle is true of our Heavenly Father also. He desires that we—mankind—fit into His pattern of perfection. In fact, He commands it:

"Be ye therefore perfect, even as your Father which is in heaven is perfect." (Matthew 5:48.)

But is that possible? By all means, yes, through the gospel. The Lord gave us both His gospel and His Church as the means of achieving this result.

"And he gave some, apostles; and some, prophets; and some, evangelists; and some, pastors and teachers;

"For the perfecting of the saints, for the work of the ministry, for the edifying of the body of Christ:

"Till we all come in the unity of the faith, and of the knowledge of the Son of God, unto a perfect man, unto the measure of the stature of the fulness of Christ:

"That we henceforth be no more children, tossed to and fro, and carried about with every wind of doctrine, by the sleight of men, and cunning craftiness, whereby they lie in wait to deceive." (Ephesians 4:11-14.)

What a different view of ourselves is provided by this doctrine of the Fatherhood of God.

We did not arise from some lower form of life. We have been persons from the beginning. We were created as such. Christ was the firstborn of God's spirit children. We came later. In that primeval existence Christ, then known as Jehovah, became like His Father. He spoke of it here on earth. "He that hath seen me hath seen the Father." (John 14:9.) He was the "image of the invisible God," (Colossians 1:15) and "the express image of his person." (Hebrews 1:3.)

But Jesus also was in the image of human beings. He was so much like His apostles in appearance that the crucifiers could not pick Him out from among them. They had to bribe Judas to identify Him so that they would not crucify the wrong man.

All that being the case, He still was in the image of God's person. (Hebrews 1:3.) Like God—like man! And how could this be?

Because man was created in the image and likeness of God. (Genesis 1:26-27.) Christ could be no other than like both God and man since He and we are the children of God, and both He and we are in the image and likeness of God.

This doctrine becomes a mark of identification of the true Church. Man cannot be other than in the image of God. Christ could not be other than in the likeness of the Father both as to His spirit and His fleshly body. All humanity is made in the physical likeness of God. The Father is a *person*. Christ is a person. Man is a person.

Genesis also points out that as man was made in the image of God, meaning Adam, so Adam had a son in his own image and likeness. His name was Seth. So Seth resembled Adam, and Adam resembled God. Hence Seth also resembled God in appearance, and so do all the rest of us, since we are all descended from Adam, and all life was commanded to reproduce "after his kind." (Genesis 1:21, 25.)

It is significant that the scripture uses the same language to describe the resemblance of Seth to Adam as is used in describing the likeness of Adam to God. Seth was a person. Adam was a person. God is a person. (Hebrews 1:3.) It is all very significant.

The Savior commands that we become like Him in our innermost souls, in the character we shall develop, in what we say and do and think. He says that we are to become perfect as He is, as His Father is also. He gave us the gospel and the Church organization as the means of achieving that goal.

The Savior is our pattern of life. That is why He commands us to become like Him in living perfect lives. Our ultimate destiny is to become like the Father and the Son. We are not predestined to annihilation, but to live eternally.

Yes, we can become like God, but that would not be possible if we were not His children and if we were not in His image and likeness. The spark of divinity bequeathed to us by being His offspring makes it all possible.

Playing harps and singing praises to God were not intended to be our eternal occupation. Nothing like it. We are to grow and learn and develop in intelligence and powers and skills to the point where some time in eternity we will become like Him. It is all possible because we are His children and, therefore, in His likeness, and that likeness will become a true "evolution" as we achieve this great goal in the eternities.

One of the Lord's great blessings in this regard is that He gives to us the Gift of the Holy Ghost. And what does that gift do for us? It helps us on the way to perfection.

Said the Savior:

"But the Comforter, which is the Holy Ghost, whom the Father will send in my name, he shall teach you all things, and bring all things to your remembrance, whatsoever I have said unto you." (John 14:26.)

He also said:

"Howbeit when he, the Spirit of truth, is come, he will guide you into all truth: for he shall not speak of himself; but whatsoever he shall hear, that shall he speak: and he will shew you things to come.

"He shall glorify me: for he shall receive of mine, and shall shew it unto you.

"All things that the Father hath are mine: therefore said I, that he shall take of mine, and shall shew it unto you." (John 16:13-15.)

The Holy Ghost is a *revelator*. Through Him modern current

revelation comes to the Church and its prophets. But also He is a personal guide to us in our own daily lives. He will *teach* us the things of the Lord, and will keep fresh in our minds the precious truths of salvation. Indeed, the work of the Holy Ghost becomes one of the major marks of identification of the true Church.

This is why Paul wrote to the Corinthians:

"But God hath revealed them unto us by his Spirit: for the Spirit searcheth all things, yea, the deep things of God.

"For what man knoweth the things of a man, save the spirit of man which is in him? even so the things of God knoweth no man, but the Spirit of God." (1 Corinthians 2:10-11.)

Then is not the Holy Ghost a *revelator*?

Paul goes on:

"Now we have received, not the spirit of the world, but the spirit which is of God; that we might know the things that are freely given to us of God.

"Which things also we speak, not in the words which man's wisdom teacheth, but which the Holy Ghost teacheth; comparing spiritual things with spiritual." (1 Corinthians 2:12-13.)

He is a teacher, He is a guide, He is a revelator. Without Him and without His precious ministry, there would be no true Church of Christ in this age. What a great mark of identification!

How do we gain a testimony that Jesus is really the Christ? It is by the Spirit of Revelation, the Holy Ghost. Did not Peter obtain his testimony by revelation? (Matthew 16:13-19.) And did not Peter write?:

"Knowing this first, that no prophecy of the scripture is of any private interpretation.

"For the prophecy came not in old time by the will of man: but holy men of God spake as they were moved by the Holy Ghost." (2 Peter 1:20-21.)

In these modern times, as the Lord established His true Church on earth, once again He said about the Holy Ghost:

"Wherefore, I now send upon you another Comforter, even upon you my friends, that it may abide in your hearts, even the Holy Spirit of promise; which other Comforter is the same that I promised unto my disciples, as is recorded in the testimony of John.

"This Comforter is the promise which I give unto you of eternal life, even the glory of the celestial kingdom;

"Which glory is that of the church of the Firstborn, even of God, the holiest of all, through Jesus Christ his Son." (D & C 88:3-5.)

Then He spoke of the light which emanates from the Godhead, known as the Light of Christ. It is different from the person of the Holy Ghost. It is described in this way:

"This is the light of Christ. As also he is in the sun, and the light of the sun, and the power thereof by which it was made.

"As also he is in the moon, and is the light of the moon, and the power thereof by which it was made;

"As also the light of the stars, and the power thereof by which they were made;

"And the earth also, and the power thereof, even the earth upon which you stand.

"And the light which shineth, which giveth you light, is through him who enlighteneth your eyes, which is the same light that quickeneth your understandings;

"Which light proceedeth forth from the presence of God to fill the immensity of space—

"The light which is in all things, which giveth life to all things, which is the law by which all things are governed, even the power of God who sitteth upon his throne, who is in the bosom of eternity, who is in the midst of all things." (D & C 88:7-13.)

This is the doctrine of the Godhead which characterizes the true Church and is one of its marks of identification. This makes the true Church a living, vital thing, something which can make us all the disciples of Jesus.

The separateness of the members of the Godhead was nowhere more clearly demonstrated than in the First Vision of the Prophet Joseph Smith in which both Father and Son descended from heaven and appeared to the boy prophet. And what did the Prophet say?

"I saw *two* Personages, whose brightness and glory defy all description, standing above me in the air. *One* of them spake unto me, calling me by name and said, pointing *to the other*—This is my Beloved Son. Hear Him!

"...I asked the *personages* who stood above me in the light . . . . and the *personage who addressed me* . . . ." (Joseph Smith 1:17-19. Italics added.)

Joseph saw our Eternal Father and His Son Jesus Christ. They were two separate *personages,* as separate as any father and son could be.

The Holy Ghost is the third member of the Godhead, a personage of spirit, but a personage nonetheless. He, with the Father, and Jesus Christ, the Son, constitute the Godhead—a Trinity made of three distinct divine Persons, the Father, the Son, and the Holy Ghost.

Chapter Seven

Its Organization

W ho, knowing the facts, could possibly doubt that the true Church anciently had a definite organizational structure, specially designated officers, and a clear-cut program of operation?

And who, knowing the facts, could wonder that such an organization would in and of itself constitute a major mark of identification by which anyone may satisfactorily identify that Church?

And who, again knowing the facts, could fail to see that a great apostasy took place in Christendom, and that the resultant churches, with their varied organizations and conflicting creeds, indeed have drifted far away from almost every semblance of the original Church?

Beyond any question, the Savior did organize a Church when He was on earth, and He set it up in such a way that it could endure forever if the people proved faithful. Apostasy of course could wipe it out. But He did organize a Church. As Paul so clearly pointed out, that Church was headed by apostles and prophets who formed its very foundation, supported by Christ Himself as the chief cornerstone. (Ephesians 2:20.)

But the Church had more than apostles and prophets. Many other officers made up the structure to enable it to reach all believers and potential believers.

The Savior appointed some officers in addition to the apostles during His mortal lifetime. Still others were added later under the inspiration of heaven as the word spread in that first century. The apostles, who were the seers and revelators of the Church, fully organized the work.

While He was still on earth in mortality, the Savior appointed a group of missionaries whom He called the Seventy. They were different from the Seventy in the days of Moses (Numbers 11:16; Exodus 24:1-9) who labored within the law of Moses. The new Christian Seventies labored in a situation entirely different from theirs.

The Seventy called by the Savior were missionaries, preachers of the word, who went abroad very much as did the Twelve.

"After these things the Lord appointed other seventy also, and sent them two and two before his face into every city and place, whither he himself would come.

"Therefore said he unto them, The harvest truly is great, but the labourers are few: pray ye therefore the Lord of the harvest, that he would send forth labourers into his harvest.

"Go your ways: behold, I send you forth as lambs among wolves.

"Carry neither purse, nor scrip, nor shoes: and salute no man by the way.

"And into whatsoever house ye enter, first say, Peace be to this house.

"And if the son of peace be there, your peace shall rest upon it: if not, it shall turn to you again.

"And in the same house remain, eating and drinking such things as they give: for the labourer is worthy of his hire. Go not from house to house.

"And into whatsoever city ye enter, and they receive you, eat such things as are set before you:

"And heal the sick that are therein, and say unto them, The kingdom of God is come nigh unto you.

"But into whatsoever city ye enter, and they receive you not, go your ways out into the streets of the same, and say,

"Even the very dust of your city, which cleaveth on us, we do wipe off against you: notwithstanding be ye sure of this, that the kingdom of God is come nigh unto you.

"But I say unto you, that it shall be more tolerable in that day for Sodom, than for that city." (Luke 10:1-12.)

The similarity between the call given to them and that given to the Twelve—both by the Savior—is obvious and remarkable. (See Matthew 10.) Although their call as missionaries resembled that of the Twelve, their authority was less. However, they did have power to perform miracles.

When they returned from their first missionary journey, they rejoiced as they reported to the Lord.

"And the seventy returned again with joy, saying, Lord, even the devils are subject unto us through thy name.

"And he said unto them, I beheld Satan as lightning fall from heaven.

"Behold, I give unto you power to tread on serpents and scorpions, and over all the power of the enemy: and nothing shall by any means hurt you.

"Notwithstanding in this rejoice not, that the spirits are subject unto you; but rather rejoice, because your names are written in heaven." (Luke 10:17-20.)

What church can match this Quorum of Seventy today? In what denomination may we find even a remote reflection of the Seventies' divine commission? Such a quorum is unique to the Church of Jesus Christ, and is a major mark of identification of that Church. If this quorum is lacking, "where were the body?" Without seventies, where is the Church?

They are an integral part of "the body of Christ," and since the hand cannot say to the foot, "I have no need of thee," would any officer in the true Church dare say to the Seventy, "I have no need of thee?" And yet, where are they in Christendom? Without the Seventy, where is the Church of Jesus Christ?

There were still other officers in that early Church. They were evangelists, pastors, teachers, deacons, priests, elders, and bishops. They, too, were parts of the "body of Christ," and were fitly joined together, each one in its proper capacity.

They were functional officers of the Church quite as much as were the apostles and prophets, for not even the head (apostles) can say to what seems to be the least extremity of the body (deacons), "I have no need of thee."

Paul spoke of high priests (Hebrews 5). Evangelists, pastors, and teachers are mentioned in Ephesians 4:11-14. Elders were ordained "in every church." (Acts 14:23; 15:6; 1 Peter 5:1.)

Instructions were given in detail to the bishops of that day (1 Timothy 3:1-11), and deacons received their commissions with similar teachings. (1 Timothy 3:12.)

Timothy, one of those bishops, lived at Lystra (Acts 16:1) but later was stationed at Ephesus. He was born of a Jewish mother and a Grecian father. He fought a valiant fight against the apostasy which seeped into Ephesus.

Titus lived in Crete and was bishop there. A reading of Paul's epistle to him reveals the problems which faced the branch of the Church on that island.

With priests it was much like it was with the elders. There were both priests and elders under the Law of Moses, but now both elders and priests were placed in the Church of Jesus Christ as parts of the new regime. The law of Moses was fulfilled by the Savior (3 Nephi 15) and with the coming of the gospel, new ordinances and teachings were introduced. This meant new officers and new duties for these men to perform. The gospel opened a whole new day, with these new teachings and new officers who were required to administer the affairs of the Church.

Both prophets and teachers are mentioned in Acts 13, where we read of the callings that came to Saul of Tarsus and Barnabas, his friend.

But transcending all of these officers were the Twelve Apostles. They were placed at the head of the Church, and were expected to remain there for the following reasons:

1. They were the foundation of the Church. (Ephesians 2:20.)

2. Their responsibility was the perfecting of the Saints, the work of the ministry, and the edifying of the body of Christ. (Ephesians 4:11-12.)

3. They were to remain in the Church to preserve a "unity of the faith." (Ephesians 4:13.)

4. They were to protect the members from false teachers. (Ephesians 4:14-16.)

5. They were commissioned to preach the gospel worldwide. (Matthew 28:19-20.)

Dr. James E. Talmage explains further:

"Besides these specific offices in the Priesthood, there were other callings of a more temporal nature, to which men were also set apart by authority; such for instance was the case of the seven men of honest report who, in the days of the apostles, were appointed to minister to the poor, thus leaving the Twelve freer to attend to the particular duties of their office. This special appointment illustrates the nature of the helps and governments set in the Church, to assist in the work under the direction of the regular officers of the Priesthood.

"The ministers so appointed and the members among whom they labor constitute the Church of Christ, which has been impressively compared to a perfect body, the individuals typifying the separate members, each with its own functions, all cooperating for the welfare of the whole. Every office so established, every officer so commissioned, is necessary to the development of the Church and to the accomplishment of its work. An organization established of God comprises no superfluities; the eye, the ear, the hand, the foot, every organ of the body, is essential to the symmetry and perfection of the physical structure; in the Church no officer can rightly say to another: 'I have no need of thee.'

"The existence of these officers, and particularly their operation with accompaniments of divine assistance and power, may be taken as a distinguishing characteristic of the Church in any age of the world—a crucial test, whereby the validity or falsity of any claim to divine authority may be determined. The Gospel of Jesus Christ is the everlasting Gospel; its principles, laws and ordinances, and the Church organization founded thereon, must be ever the same. In searching for the true Church, therefore, one must look for an organization comprising the offices established of old, the callings of apostles, prophets, evangelists, high priests, seventies, pastors, bishops, elders, priests, teachers, deacons—not men bearing these names merely, but ministers able to vindicate their claim to position as officers in the Lord's service, through the evidences of power and authority accompanying their ministry." (*Articles of Faith*, Deseret Book Co., pp. 198-199.)

Chapter Eight

Members Called Saints

How were the members of the early Church known to each other, that is, by what name? Did they call themselves Christians, after Christ? What was their name?

Scripture indicates that they were first called Christians in the very anti-Christ and idolatrous community of Antioch. They were called thus in derision. (Acts 11:26.) When Paul stood before Agrippa, who was allied with those who were persecuting the disciples, the king said: "Almost thou persuadest me to be a Christian." (Acts 26:28.) He used the hated term by which the disciples were known among their persecutors.

Peter referred to this persecution of the hated Christians when he wrote: "If any man suffer as a Christian, let him not be ashamed; but let him glorify God on this behalf." (1 Peter 4:16.)

Jesus said: "Blessed are they which are persecuted for righteousness' sake: for theirs is the kingdom of heaven. Blessed are ye, when men shall revile you, and persecute you, and shall say all manner of evil against you falsely, for my sake. Rejoice, and be exceeding glad: for great is your reward in heaven: for so persecuted they the prophets which were before you." (Matthew 5:10-12.)

Jesus was bitterly hated in Palestine by most of the people, Romans, Greeks, and Jews alike. Only a few faithful converts knew Him as their Lord and their God.

Hence, the name of Christ became an epithet in the mouths of many in that day, and the persecutors sought to show their bitterness toward the followers of Christ by calling them after Him. Since His name was used by them in derision, also in derision these evil people called His disciples Christians. They sought to place upon the humble worshippers of Christ the badge of hate, so they called them Christians. Bearing the name of Christ in a world of hate, those believers did so humbly and gratefully, for they knew He was their Lord and Savior.

But what did the disciples call themselves? They were known to each other as Saints. This was a designation that was used among the people of God in both Old and New Testaments.

Moses spoke of them by this name. (Deuteronomy 33:2-3.) They are referred to in Samuel's writings (1 Samuel 2:9), and in the Psalms. (Psalms 50, 89, 97, 149.)

In Daniel we find the name (Daniel 7:18, 22, 27). Zechariah referred to it in prophecy. (Zechariah 14:5.)

Paul addressed his epistles to the Saints who lived in the various cities to which he sent his messages. (Romans 1:7; 8:27; 12:13; 15:25.)

In 1 Corinthians we find the expression repeatedly as the apostle speaks to the disciples by that name. (1 Corinthians 1:2; 6:2; 14:33.) He does so in 2 Corinthians, also, and similarly in Ephesians.

There it was that he spoke of perfecting and edifying the Saints. (Ephesians 4:12.) He opened that epistle with this expression: "To the saints which are at Ephesus," welcoming the newcomers to the fold with this expression:

"Now therefore ye are no more strangers and foreigners, but fellow-citizens with the saints, and of the household of God;

"And are built upon the foundation of the apostles and prophets, Jesus Christ himself being the chief corner stone." (Ephesians 2:19-20.)

He called himself the "least of all saints." (Ephesians 3:8.) He spoke of abstaining from immorality "as becometh saints." (Ephesians 5:3.)

He addressed the Colossians as "saints and faithful brethren." (Colossians 1:2.) He saluted the Hebrew saints (Hebrews 13:24), and Jude spoke of the evil forces which contended with the Saints. (Jude 1:4.)

John the Revelator referred to the prayers of the Saints as being pleasing to the Lord. (Revelation 5:8; 8:3.) He also spoke of the patience and faith of the Saints (Revelation 13:10; 14:12) and referred to the martyred Saints. (Revelation 16:6.) He told of attacks upon the Saints as their enemies encamped about them. (Revelation 20:9.)

Webster's dictionary says that the term "saints" was the name by which the early Christians were known among themselves. Similar definitions are provided in Bible dictionaries.

There is no question about it: the disciples in the early Church called themselves *saints.* This becomes one of the marks of identification of the true Church. It is not the only one, of course, but it is *one,* and must be included in any description of "the body of Christ."

The people were not called after any leader among them, not after Peter or James or John, not after Paul or Apollos (1 Corinthians 1:12), and not after any geographical location. They were called simply by the expression *saints.*

In what church today is this a common designation for its members?

Chapter Nine

Called As Was Aaron

In what manner did the ministers of Christ receive their calls and authority? The correct method becomes one of the outstanding signs of the true Church.

A specific call, in a precise manner, was vital. Did not the Lord warn against false prophets and false Christs? (Matthew 24.) And did He not denounce the false creeds of men? (Matthew 15:9.) He said that such teachings were utterly in vain.

How were men to be called to the ministry of Christ? Here is Paul's definition:

"No man taketh this honour unto himself, but he that is called of God, as was Aaron." (Hebrews 5:4.)

Some argue that this is not a proper translation of the scripture. However, modern versions sustain King James fully:

The New English Bible:

"And nobody arrogates this honor to himself; he is called by God as indeed Aaron was."

Revised Standard Version:

"And one does not take the honor upon himself, but is called by God just as Aaron was."

Knox Version:

"His vocation comes from God; nobody can take on himself such a privilege as this."

Philips:

"Note also that nobody chooses for himself the honor of being a high priest, but he is called by God to the work as was Aaron."

Moffatt:

"It is an office which no one elects to take for himself; he is called to it by God, just as Aaron was."

Note how in these cases the wording is: called *by God*. Is that not significant?

Aaron's call came in this way:

"And take thou unto thee Aaron thy brother, and his sons with him, from among the children of Israel, that he may minister unto me in the priest's office, even Aaron, Nadab and Abihu, Eleazar and Ithamar, Aaron's sons." (Exodus 28:1.)

Then what was the method?

God gave a revelation to His living prophet, designating the men whom He would have serve in the ministry. It was current revelation to a living prophet.

As Paul pointed this out to the Hebrews in the Church of Jesus Christ, he prescribed it as the pattern by which all of God's ministers were to be called, giving the pattern for the "body of Christ." The procedure was no different from the calls prior to that day because God does not change His method of calling men to the priesthood. It must be by revelation through the proper priesthood authority—a prophet.

When men are *not* called in this manner, are they truly called of God? If they should baptize a person, would that ordinance be valid? God's ways are not man's ways.

The method of appointing men by revelation is shown even more clearly in the fortieth chapter of Exodus. Since it is available to all in the King James Version, we quote here only from some of the new translations. Note the detail by which the Lord instructs Moses:

Standard Revised Version:

"Then you shall bring Aaron and his sons to the door of the tent of meeting, and shall wash them with water and put upon Aaron the holy garment and you shall anoint and consecrate him that he may serve me as priest. You shall bring his sons also and anoint them as you anointed their father that they may serve me as priests."

Knox Catholic Version:

"Bring Aaron too, and his sons, to the doors of the Taber-nacle...and when they have washed, clothe them with sacred vestments in which they are to minister to me, and anoint them to be my priests."

Moffatt:

"...After bathing them with water put sacred robes on Aaron, anoint him and consecrate him to serve me as priest. Bring his sons, put on their tunics, and anoint them as you did their father, that they may serve me as priests."

Most significantly, the Lord followed this same pattern for the successors of Aaron. No wonder Paul stressed this unchangeable method, even for his day.

When Aaron was about to die, the Lord—again through his living prophet Moses—made arrangements for succession in that priesthood calling. It is recorded in the King James Version as follows:

"Take Aaron and Eleazar his son, and bring them up unto mount Hor:

"And strip Aaron of his garments, and put them upon Eleazar his son: and Aaron shall be gathered unto his people, and shall die there.

"And Moses did as the Lord commanded: and they went up into mount Hor in the sight of all the congregation.

"And Moses stripped Aaron of his garments, and put them upon Eleazar his son; and Aaron died there in the top of the mount: and Moses and Eleazar came down from the mount." (Numbers 20:25-28.)

As one additional example, taken from the modern versions, we have this from Knox:

"Take Aaron and his son with thee to the top of Mount Hor, strip the father of his priestly garments and clothe Eleazar his son with them instead; there Aaron shall die....So Moses did as the Lord bade him."

Again the calling of a man to priestly office was by and through the living prophet. Revelation—at the very time—was re-quired. It could not arise out of an assumption from some book—not even from the Bible, because the Bible possesses no priestly authority. It is but a printed record.

No seminary, no election, no self-suggestion can substitute for God's plan which is not subject to change. Paul understood the process very well. Note this:

"Now there were in the church that was at Antioch certain prophets and teachers; as Barnabas, and Simeon that was called Niger, and Lucius of Cyrene, and Manaen, which had been brought up with Herod the tetrarch, and Saul.

"As they ministered to the Lord, and fasted, the Holy Ghost said, Separate me Barnabas and Saul for the work whereunto I have called them.

"And when they had fasted and prayed, and laid their hands on them, they sent them away.

"So they, being sent forth by the Holy Ghost, departed unto Seleucia; and from thence they sailed to Cyprus." (Acts 13:1-4.)

The prophets of the Church were assembled with the teachers. During their meeting, they received a revelation by the power of the Holy Ghost specifically calling Saul of Tarsus and his friend and benefactor Barnabas. After receiving their instructions by this revelation, the prophets laid their hands upon the two men and ordained them to their callings. "So they, being sent forth by the Holy Ghost, departed." Both men possessed the apostolic powers. (Acts 14:4, 14.)

It is interesting that when Paul spoke subsequently of his calling, he wrote to the Galatians:

"But I certify you, brethren, that the gospel which was preached of me is not after man.

"For I neither received it of man, neither was I taught it, but by the revelation of Jesus Christ." (Galatians 1:11-12.)

In regard to the calling of Paul and Barnabas as set forth in Acts, thirteenth chapter, it is significant that new translations of the Bible use the expression "set apart."

The Schoenfeld Bible says, "The Holy Spirit said, Set apart for me, Barnabas and Saul for the task I have assigned to them."

The New English Bible says:

"Set Barnabas and Saul apart for me to do the work to which I have called them."

The Standard Revised Version:

"The Holy Spirit said: Set apart for me Barnabas and Saul for the work to which I have called them."

Where else but in the Lord's Church are men "set apart" to their priestly duties?

When Jesus described the call He extended to His apostles, He said:

"Ye have not chosen me, but I have chosen you, and ordained you, that ye should go and bring forth fruit, and that your fruit should remain: that whatsoever ye shall ask of the Father in my name, he may give it you." (John 15:16.)

In this instance He officiated for himself, since He was on earth personally, and hence did not require the use of revelation. After His ascension, of course, revelation was needed, and it had to come through living prophets.

Would the Lord call His servants in any other way? What did the Prophet Amos say about the Lord's method of operation?

"Surely the Lord God will do nothing, but he revealeth his secret unto his servants the prophets." (Amos 3:7.)

Would God call his ministers in any other way?

This procedure, then, becomes one of the great signs of the true Church. Its ministers must be called through revelation with the services of a living prophet—even as was Aaron.

Chapter Ten

Additional Scripture

Another of the signs of the true Church is that it always will produce new and additional scripture.

Startling to many people who believe that the Bible contains it all, the fact remains: new scripture must be part and parcel of the true Church. Why?

How did the Bible come into existence? Where did these various writings, now contained in one well-bound volume, come from?

Each book is the record of the revelations and ministry, and some history at times, of the prophet whose name it bears.

Since the Lord will do nothing except through His prophets, He provided prophets to the earth whenever He had a people whom He recognized as His own.

This was true in the days of Enoch and Noah, Abraham, Isaac and Jacob, Moses, Elijah, Jeremiah, Isaiah, Micah and all the rest.

Not all of these prophets wrote books, but events in their lives are recorded by other writers.

The fact is that with succeeding prophets, additional books of scripture were provided. Each prophet was a minister of God. Each received direction by revelation. As these revelations were recorded together with the history of the man's ministry, they became scripture. Many of these writings were added to the existing volume of scripture when published. Some of the early scriptures have never been found and are still missing.

Moses wrote the first five books of the Bible. Then Joshua was called to the work. The record says:

"And Joshua the son of Nun was full of the spirit of wisdom; for Moses had laid his hands upon him: and the children of Israel hearkened unto him, and did as the Lord commanded Moses." (Deuteronomy 34:9.)

When the Lord spoke to this new prophet about his work, He promised: "As I was with Moses, so I will be with thee: I will not fail thee, nor forsake thee." (Joshua 1:5.)

The book of Joshua recorded his activities under the direction of the Lord. Full of revelation and history, it was added to the existing volume of scripture—meaning the five books of Moses—and became scripture itself. There were now six books of scripture instead of five.

So it was with other succeeding prophets. Hence appeared the books of Samuel, the book of Nehemiah, of Isaiah, of Jeremiah, of Ezekiel, of Daniel, of Malachi, and the others.

These books were added to the existing volume of scripture, and became part of Holy Writ, evidencing that scripture is a growing thing, growing with the prophets who provided it.

The same thing held true with the New Testament. We have the four Gospels and the Acts, but then we have the inspirational letters of Paul, and James and John and Peter and Jude, and the writings contained in the Revelation of John on Patmos. They were not all written at the same time. They were provided over the years as the work progressed.

Since the Church must be directed by the Lord, and He gives His revelation to His prophets, since prophets and revelation must ever be in the true Church, and since those revelations and sacred histories are recorded and are added to the existing Holy Writ, we accept them as scripture.

In the true Church there will be new revelation. Hence, the true Church will produce new and additional scripture. It is one of the signs to guide us as we search for the truth.

Chapter Eleven

Admission to the Church

The manner in which we become members of Christ's true Church is itself a mark of identification to be correctly recognized.

There exists a definite procedure, and to vary from it is to depart from the way of the Lord.

How may a person join the true Church?

The first step is acceptance of Jesus as the Christ, as the literal and divine Son of God, recognizing Him as our Savior and our Redeemer. We acknowledge, too, that He is the Creator of all things, as the scripture says.

Next we must study His gospel, His ways, His requirements for salvation, and, as He Himself said, "Learn of me."

He taught us to "search the scriptures" (John 5:39) and take upon us His yoke:

"Come unto me, all ye that labour and are heavy laden, and I will give you rest.

"Take my yoke upon you, and learn of me; for I am meek and lowly in heart: and ye shall find rest unto your souls.

"For my yoke is easy, and my burden is light." (Matthew 11:28-30.)

Then comes the next principle as set forth by Peter in a most decisive manner:

"Then Peter said unto them, Repent, and be baptized every one of you in the name of Jesus Christ for the remission of sins, and ye shall receive the gift of the Holy Ghost.

"For the promise is unto you, and to your children, and to all that are afar off, even as many as the Lord our God shall call." (Acts 2:38-39.)

Repentance is all-essential, of course. No unclean thing may come into His presence. We must be cleansed of the sins of the world as we may have participated in them.

John the Baptist vigorously preached repentance. Jesus Himself began His ministry with: "Repent: for the kingdom of heaven is at hand." (Matthew 4:17.) The apostles did the same, for after their call "they went out, and preached that men should repent." (Mark 6:12.)

It was Peter who said:

"Repent ye therefore, and be converted, that your sins may be blotted out, when the time of refreshing shall come from the presence of the Lord." (Acts 3:19.)

There is no more emphatic commandment in the gospel of the Lord Jesus Christ than that of baptism by immersion for the remission of sins.

When the Lord came to John the Baptist and requested baptism, He set at rest all question of whether it is an essential saving ordinance:

"For thus it becometh us to fulfill all righteousness" was His declaration. (Matthew 3:15.)

"To fulfill all righteousness." Then all righteousness could neither be satisfied nor fulfilled without that ordinance. Is it any wonder then that He sent His apostles out "to all the world" to both preach and baptize? The salvation or damnation of human souls would be determined by their compliance with or rejection of this law! Then can baptism be ignored or brushed aside any more than faith?

As Matthew records it, He said:

"Go ye therefore, and teach all nations, baptizing them in the name of the Father, and of the Son, and of the Holy Ghost:

"Teaching them to observe all things whatsoever I have commanded you: and, lo, I am with you alway, even unto the end of the world. Amen." (Matthew 28:19-20.)

Is there any uncertainty in that? Are there any loopholes by which anyone might escape the necessity of complying with this law?

"Go," He said.

"Teach," He said.

"Baptize," He said.

And the ordinance must be performed in the name of the entire Godhead in Heaven—the Father, and the Son, and the Holy Ghost. Could there be anything more important or sacred? Dare anyone set aside an ordinance prescribed by the divine Trinity?

Mark recorded it thus:

"And he said unto them, Go ye into all the world, and preach the gospel to every creature.

"He that believeth and is baptized shall be saved; but he that believeth not shall be damned.

"And these signs shall follow them that believe; In my name shall they cast out devils; they shall speak with new tongues;

"They shall take up serpents; and if they drink any deadly thing, it shall not hurt them: they shall lay hands on the sick, and they shall recover." (Mark 16:15-18.)

Those who believed would be baptized. That was His order. Those who did not believe sufficiently to accept baptism "shall be damned."

How dare anyone discard baptism? And yet some do. This ordinance is excluded from some so-called Christian creeds, and particularly from those which teach salvation by a mere confession of belief.

Do they not remember that faith without works is dead? (James 2:26.)

Do they not remember that the Savior said His followers should do "the works that I do," and was He not baptized? (John 14:12.)

Sin is another consideration. Baptism is for the remission of sins. Who can expect to enter the kingdom without first being cleansed of His sins?

But the cleansing does not come by any mere confession of belief either at the mercy seat, in some auditorium, or at the side of a radio or television set.

Remission of sins comes *through repentance and baptism.* It was so taught by John the Baptist. It was preached and practiced by the Savior Himself, and by the apostles who performed more baptisms than John.

"Jesus and his disciples [came] into the land of Judea; and there he tarried with them, and baptized." (John 3:22.) It is of note that "Jesus made and baptized more disciples than John." (John 4:1-2.)

"The publicans, justified God, being baptized with the baptism of John. But the Pharisees and lawyers *rejected the counsel of God against themselves, being not baptized of him.*" (Luke 7:29-30. Italics added.)

Then what of people today who reject baptism? Do they not also reject the counsel of God against themselves? The counsel of God is "be baptized."

This passage is significant:

"Now when they heard this, they were pricked in their heart, and said unto Peter and to the rest of the apostles, Men and brethren, what shall we do?

"Then Peter said unto them, Repent, and be baptized every one of you in the name of Jesus Christ for the remission of sins, and ye shall receive the gift of the Holy Ghost." (Acts 2:37-38.)

Many references certify that baptism is for the remission of sins. Note, for example, this relating to the baptism of Saul of Tarsus:

"And now why tarriest thou? arise, and be baptized, and wash away thy sins, calling on the name of the Lord." (Acts 22:16.)

"Be baptized and wash away thy sins." And he obeyed this command. Should not we?

"And Ananias went his way, and entered into the house; and putting his hands on him said, Brother Saul, the Lord, even Jesus, that appeared unto thee in the way as thou camest, hath sent me, that thou mightest receive thy sight, and be filled with the Holy Ghost.

"And immediately there fell from his eyes as it had been scales: and he received sight forthwith, and arose, and was baptized.

"And when he had received meat, he was strengthened. Then was Saul certain days with the disciples which were at Damascus.

"And straightway he preached Christ in the synagogues, that he is the Son of God." (Acts 9:17-20.)

It was the case also with Cornelius:

"Can any man forbid water, that these should not be baptized, which have received the Holy Ghost as well as we?

"And he commanded them to be baptized in the name of the Lord. Then prayed they him to tarry certain days." (Acts 10:47-48.)

There is no question but that baptism is an essential saving ordinance. No one who is willing to accept the facts will deny that through baptism our sins are remitted.

Then can churches that deny the need for baptism, saying that sins are remitted by mere confession, lay any valid claim to being the true Church?

Baptism for the remission of sins—when properly done—is one of the vital marks of identification of the true Church. It is only one, but it is one. It is not "the whole body" but it is an essential part that must be there.

But baptism has another use also. It is the doorway into the Church, the means of taking upon ourselves the name of Christ.

To Nicodemus, Jesus explained this important fact: We are born of the water and the Spirit to "enter into the kingdom of God." (John 3:5.) It is the gateway.

Paul taught the Romans that we are "baptized into Jesus Christ." Is not that admittance to His kingdom? (Romans 6:3.)

He told the Corinthians we are "baptized into one body," that is, His Church. (1 Corinthians 12:13.) Baptism is the means by which we join His Church and become members "with the saints, and of the household of God." (Ephesians 2:19.) Then is baptism necessary? Why do people misunderstand?

Since it is so essential, how should it be performed? By what mode?

Not only did baptism provide remission of sins to the repentant soul, and admit him "into Christ," it had a special symbolism which was important, and which gives us the mode of performing the ordinance.

Just as the sacrament of the Lord's Supper is symbolic of the Crucifixion, so baptism is the symbol of His burial and resurrection. It had to be by immersion because it represented both the burial of the Savior, and His subsequent coming forth in the

Resurrection. Doesn't this all give further evidence that baptism is an essential saving ordinance?

As Christ was buried in the tomb, we are buried in the water, and as He came forth from the grave, we come forth from the "watery grave" of baptism. Nothing else provides that symbolism, a *reminder* to us of the death and resurrection of Christ, just as the broken bread and the sacred cup are reminders of the suffering on the cross. It is just as essential as the sacrament of the Lord's Supper.

Paul explained this "burial" to the Colossians, when he wrote:

"Buried with him in baptism, wherein also ye are risen with him through the faith of the operation of God, who hath raised him from the dead." (Colossians 2:12.)

He taught the same thing to the Romans:

"Know ye not, that so many of us as were baptized into Jesus Christ were baptized into his death?

"Therefore we are buried with him by baptism into death: that like as Christ was raised up from the dead by the glory of the Father, even so we also should walk in newness of life.

"For if we have been planted together in the likeness of his death, we shall be also in the likeness of his resurrection." (Romans 6:3-5.)

Then baptism is likened both to a "planting" and a "burial." Clearly, immersion is the only mode. The very word baptize means to immerse.

But there is one more element. The baptism must be performed by one properly authorized to do so.

Who baptized in the days of the Savior? John the Baptist was the first. He was "sent" for this purpose:

"And I knew him not: but *he that sent me to baptize with water*, the same said unto me. . . ." (John 1:33. Italics added.)

Can anyone doubt John's authority when even the Savior submitted to it? Could Jesus accept baptism from an unauthorized person? Would that have fulfilled all righteousness?

Who else baptized? The apostles. And were they called and ordained? (John 4:1-2; 15:16; Matthew 10:1-5.) He gave them power and "sent them forth."

Ananias was "sent" to Paul to heal and baptize him. (Acts 9:10-20.)

And why was this authority to baptize limited only to those who were "sent?" Paul explained:

"And no man taketh this honour unto himself, but he that is called of God, as was Aaron." (Hebrews 5:4.)

They had to be called of God as was Aaron, which was by revelation to a living prophet, with the laying on of hands. (Acts 13:2-3; Exodus 28.)

Again, we have a vivid sign of the true Church which must provide:

Baptism in water for the remission of sins.

Baptism of "fire and the Holy Ghost."

Baptism for admittance "into Christ."

Baptism by immersion, a symbol of the Resurrection.

Baptism by one having authority, given him in the manner the priesthood was given to Aaron.

Chapter Twelve

Saving the Dead

V ery distinctive of the true Church is the Lord's method of extending salvation to the dead as well as to the living.

All mankind are children of God. The Lord is no respecter of persons. His gospel is for "every nation, kindred, tongue and people." And when He said He was the God of both living and dead, for all live unto Him (Luke 20:38), He included the dead also in His plan of salvation.

What was His plan of salvation for the dead? What was His plan for the living? Should not both be the same?

His plan of salvation for the living began with preaching the word. His plan for saving the dead also began with preaching the word to all who are in their graves. He was very emphatic in this declaration:

"Verily, verily, I say unto you, He that heareth my word, and believeth on him that sent me, hath everlasting life, and shall not come into condemnation; but is passed from death unto life." (John 5:24.)

Here is a simple definition: those who hear His voice and believe on Him shall have everlasting life.

Then He said that He would preach even to the dead:

"Verily, verily, I say unto you, The hour is coming, and now is, when the dead shall hear the voice of the Son of God: and they that hear shall live." (John 5:25.)

He reemphasized His point by declaring:

"Marvel not at this: for the hour is coming, in the which all that are in the graves shall hear his voice,

"And shall come forth; they that have done good, unto the resurrection of life; and they that have done evil, unto the resurrection of damnation." (John 5:28-29.)

But did He ever really preach to the dead in fulfillment of that passage? Most assuredly. Note what Peter says on this point:

"For Christ also hath once suffered for sins, the just for the unjust, that he might bring us to God, being put to death in the flesh, but quickened by the Spirit:

"By which also he went and preached unto the spirits in prison;

"Which sometime were disobedient, when once the longsuffering of God waited in the days of Noah, while the ark was a preparing, wherein few, that is, eight souls were saved by water." (1 Peter 3:18-20.)

Here is the message: Christ went to the dead and preached to them while His own body lay in the tomb. He was dead and so were they, yet they all *lived* in the spirit. They were able to listen and learn and *accept* His message. The gospel truly was also for them. And we certainly learn here something not generally known about the dead:

They were alert, and they could learn, even though their bodies were destroyed in the flood.

They were spirits—intelligent and teachable.

Obviously a person is a dual being: He has a spirit as well as a body in which the spirit lives in mortality. Although the body dies, the spirit lives on.

The apostles knew this, and Jesus referred to it after His own resurrection. The apostles did not at first understand the Resurrection. When Jesus emerged from the grave and appeared to them, they thought He was a spirit. They recognized Him, but could not understand about the physical resurrection.

So He spoke to His doubting apostles:

"Jesus himself stood in the midst of them, and saith unto them, Peace be unto you.

"But they were terrified and affrighted, and supposed that they had seen a spirit.

"And he said unto them, Why are ye troubled? and why do thoughts arise in your hearts?

"Behold my hands and my feet, that it is I myself: handle me, and see; for a spirit hath not flesh and bones, as ye see me have.

"And when he had thus spoken, he shewed them his hands and his feet.

"And while they yet believed not for joy, and wondered, he said unto them, Have ye here any meat?

"And they gave him a piece of a broiled fish, and of an honeycomb.

"And he took it, and did eat before them." (Luke 24:36-43.)

The point we make here is that we as human beings are dual persons; we do have spirits, and our spirits live beyond death. Through the Savior's visit to the dead, the gospel was extended even to those who died in the flood. (1 Peter 3:18-20.)

And why did He so instruct them? Would He have any other motive than to endeavor to save them? He was the *Savior.* Peter explains:

"For for this cause was the gospel preached also to them that are dead, that they might be judged according to men in the flesh, but live according to God in the spirit." (1 Peter 4:6.)

The gospel was preached to the dead that they might live according to God in the spirit world, in the region of those who have departed this life but who were still alive and alert, as we all shall be when we die.

The new translations of the Bible sustain and verify this doctrine as it is set forth in the King James version. There is no error in translation. All versions teach the same thing.

God is no respecter of persons—He treats everyone the same. Or does He? Of course He does! Then what about baptism? If baptism is essential to save the living, is it also needed to save the dead? What was it the Lord said about baptism? "For thus it becometh us to fulfill all righteousness."

The dead must fulfill all righteousness as well as the living. But how can they be given baptism? Anciently it was done by others in their behalf, vicariously.

Paul testified that baptisms for the dead were performed in his day. When he defended the doctrine of the resurrection in his brilliant epistle to the doubting Corinthians, he declared as one reason to accept the resurrection:

"Else what shall they do which are baptized for the dead, if the dead rise not at all? why are they then baptized for the dead?" (1 Corinthians 15:29.)

Some claim there is an error of translation here, and that in reality there was no such ordinance as baptism for the dead. But all the new translations reaffirm this doctrine. Paul knew what he was talking about. The Saints performed vicarious baptisms for their dead.

A verse in the New English version reads:

"Again there are those who receive baptism on behalf of the dead. Why should they do this? If the dead are not raised to life at all what do they mean by being baptized for the dead?"

The Schoenfeld Bible: "What are they doing who are immersed on behalf of the dead? If the dead are not raised, why be immersed on their behalf?"

The New American Bible (Catholic):

"If the dead are not raised what about those who have themselves baptized on behalf of the dead? If the raising of the dead is not a reality, why be baptized on their behalf?"

Jerusalem Bible (Catholic):

"If it were not true, what do people hope to gain by being baptized for the dead? If the dead are not ever going to be raised, why be bapized on their behalf?"

Moffatt version:

"Otherwise, if there is no such thing as a resurrection, what is the meaning of people getting baptized on behalf of their dead? If dead men do not rise at all, why do people get baptized on their behalf?"

Knox (Catholic):

"Tell me, what can be the use of being baptized for the dead if the dead do not rise again? Why should anyone be baptized for them?"

At the close of World War II, in 1947, the Roman Catholic Church in England published a new version of its Bible. Its rendering of the passage reads:

"Otherwise what shall they do that are baptized for the dead, if the dead rise not again at all? Why are they then baptized for them?"

This Bible has an interpretive footnote referring to that passage which says that there existed a custom, which Paul mentions, of being baptized for those who died without baptism, "vicarious baptism therefore." They here agree that the ordinance existed.

Here, then, is another sign of the true Church, which has a definite means of saving the dead, teaching that Christ brings the gospel to the departed so that they might live according to God (obeying His commandments) in the spirit world. And related to that doctrine is vicarious baptism of the living on behalf of the dead. What church on earth has such a procedure?

It is a vital sign of the true Church.

Chapter Thirteen

The Splintered Church

All will agree that Christianity today is divided into many factions and denominations. Hundreds of sects now exist as in generations past.

During the first century there were at least thirty of them. They ranged from Hellenists, who favored the intrusion of Greek philosophies into the Christian fabric, to the Herodians and the Coptics.

As the trend developed during the succeeding centuries, overwhelming evidence pointed to a complete departure from the original Church.

New creeds, new organizations, new titles and jurisdictions were created, all of which together crowded out the simple ways of the original Church and smothered in philosophy and endless speculations the simple truths that Jesus taught.

It became evident that the predictions of the scriptures foretelling such a departure were being fearfully and literally fulfilled.

When Paul complained to the Corinthians that they had lost their faith in Christ since they denied His resurrection, he was writing a chapter describing the apostasy from the truth in his own day.

When he told Timothy that "in the latter times some shall depart from the faith, giving heed to seducing spirits, and doctrines of devils" (1 Timothy 4:1) and when he told Timothy further that perilous times were soon to come when "men shall be lovers of their own selves, covetous, boasters, proud, blasphemers, disobedient to parents, unthankful, unholy, without natural affection," and that they would be traitors, fierce, despisers of those that are good (2 Timothy 3:2-4), he was forecasting what took place in reality a few short years after his time.

When he accused the Galatians of turning to a different gospel which was not a gospel at all, he exposed even further moves in opposition to the truth. (Galatians 1.)

And when the Apostle Peter wrote that false prophets already had arisen among the Saints, introducing "damnable heresies, even denying the Lord who bought them" (2 Peter 2:1), he joined Paul in laying out the proofs of apostasy.

A little later when the scriptures were withheld from the people, and it became a "sin" even to touch them, the condition was a violation of the words of the Savior Himself who commanded that the scriptures should be searched, for therein is the way of truth. (John 5:39.)

In the face of all this, it became of greatest significance that both the apostles Peter and John had foretold the restoration of the gospel. Peter said this would be a universal restoration of all that God had ever spoken through His prophets from the beginning of the world. (Acts 3:21.)

John said the restoration would come by means of an angel flying through the midst of heaven, bringing the gospel back to earth, to be preached to every nation, kindred, and tongue. (Revelation 14:6-7.)

This apostasy and the predicted restoration clearly show that sects which survived over the ages could not possibly be the true Church, for the restoration was to be a modern event, coming in "the hour of God's judgment."

The churches which arose in modern times do not qualify either, for none of them even believe in angelic visitations, certainly not the flight of one bringing back the everlasting gospel in the hour of God's judgment.

New denominations are still being formed by enterprising men who take advantage of the freedoms allowed by governments.

They write their own creeds, and set up their own liturgies, but they are just that—their own. They do not qualify under John's prophecy. (Revelation 14:6-7.)

One of the interesting facts about them is that few call their churches after the name of Christ. There are St. Paul's church, St. Peter's church, St. Matthew's church, the First Avenue Baptist church, the Church of England, the Church of Scotland, the United Church of Canada, the Adventists, the Methodist, and even Bible Students Associations, to mention a few.

They claim to speak for Christ, but why do they not have the courage to call their churches after His name?

The Church of Jesus Christ is not the church of Moses, nor of John the Baptist, nor of Peter or Paul.

The true Church of Jesus Christ will carry His name, which is not something to be hidden. He expects His true followers to take it abroad, and proclaim it, not hide it "under a bushel." Infinite power is in His name.

But even though the Church may be called after the Savior, should it not also teach His true and orthodox doctrines and accept and officiate in His approved ordinances? And should it not have divine authority and revelation? Should we not remember the lesson of Paul concerning "the body of Christ" with all its parts fitly joined together?

What do the scriptures say about the restoration of the gospel? When was it to take place and how? To whom would it be given? The Bible provides the answers.

In Jesus' day He referred to His second coming. (Matthew 24.) So did the apostles. In fact, so much was said that the people began to think it would take place within their own lifetime. It became necessary for the ancient apostles to correct such thinking and reveal the facts in the case.

For example, Paul wrote to the Thessalonians:

"Now we beseech you, brethren, by the coming of our Lord Jesus Christ, and by our gathering together unto him,

"That ye be not soon shaken in mind, or be troubled, neither by spirit, nor by word, nor by letter as from us, as that the day of Christ is at hand.

"Let no man deceive you by any means: for that day shall not come except there come a falling away first, and that man of sin be revealed, the son of perdition." (2 Thessalonians 2:1-3.)

That quotation is from the King James translation. It is interesting to see what the other translators did with this passage:

The New American Bible (Catholic) reads:

"We beg you, brothers, not to be so easily agitated or terrified . . . into believing that the day of the Lord is here. Let no one seduce you . . . since the mass apostasy has not yet occurred."

The footnote accompanying this passage says:

"They should not allow themselves to be duped into this way of thinking, for a religious apostasy is destined to precede the Lord's second coming."

The Knox Version (Catholic):

"Do not let anyone lead you astray. The apostasy must come first."

The New English Bible:

"Let no one deceive you in any way whatever. That day cannot come before the final rebellion against God."

The Schoenfeld Bible:

"It will not begin before the Defection has taken place."

In the Catholic version printed in England in 1947 a similar rendering occurs, but the footnote again is interesting: "This seems to refer to a great apostasy from the Christian faith preceding Christ's return."

The Coneybeare version: "Before that day the falling away must first have come."

Weymouth: ". . . for it cannot come unless the apostasy comes first."

Twentieth Century: "For it will not come until after the Great Apostasy."

So, the Second Coming would not take place until after this great apostasy.

But neither could it occur until after a restoration of the gospel. The Apostle Peter clearly explained that:

"Repent ye therefore, and be converted, that your sins may be blotted out, when the times of refreshing shall come from the presence of the Lord;

"And he shall send Jesus Christ, which before was preached unto you:

"Whom the heaven must receive until the times of restitution of all things, which God hath spoken by the mouth of all his holy prophets since the world began." (Acts 3:19-21.)

Note that all things are to be restored, all that had been spoken by the holy prophets from the beginning of the world, including the entire gospel, not only parts of it, but "the whole body" to use Paul's expression.

The fact that all would be restored anew definitely indicates that all had been lost. We cannot restore something that is already in place. Only a universal loss of the truth would make possible a universal restoration.

But some will say, "We teach out of the Bible. We worship the Savior; we preach the gospel." But do they? Creeds which are at variance with the scriptures cannot be said to reflect the Lord's views and practices. What of those who have abolished baptism? What of those who deny the physical resurrection? What of those who say Christ was only half-god, a demi-god as in Greek mythology?

Does religious liberty authorize men to change the teachings and ordinances of Christ, rewriting them to suit their own private notions? What mortal has the right to change the word of God?

But some have taken that liberty. Substitute gospels have crowded out the original in the past. We are in a situation now much like Paul found among the Galatians when he wrote:

"I marvel that ye are so soon removed from him that called you into the grace of Christ unto another gospel:

"Which is not another; but there be some that trouble you, and would pervert the gospel of Christ.

"But though we, or an angel from heaven, preach any other gospel unto you than that which we have preached unto you, let him be accursed.

"As we said before, so say I now again, If any man preach any other gospel unto you than that ye have received, let him be accursed." (Galatians 1:6-9.)

He afterward added:

"O foolish Galatians, who hath bewitched you, that ye should not obey the truth, before whose eyes Jesus Christ hath been evidently set forth, crucified among you?" (Galatians 3:1.)

Was Paul firm in his declaration that there are no substitutes for the gospel of Christ? But man-made substitutes and imitations are now widespread. The original gospel and the primitive Church disappeared. The original must be restored. God would not send His angel to earth with any other.

The people drifted away from the truth, they wrote their own creeds and their own interpretations of Holy Writ. It is a historical fact.

In a like situation, the Savior Himself denounced man-made religion and said:

"This people draweth nigh unto me with their mouth, and honoureth me with their lips; but their heart is far from me.

"But in vain they do worship me, teaching for doctrines the commandments of men." (Matthew 15:8-9.)

The translation from the Jerusalem Bible as given in Mark 7:6-9 reads this way:

"This people honors me only with lip service, while their hearts are far from me. The worship they offer me is worthless. The doctrines they teach are only human regulations."

When the Catholic Revised Standard Version appeared in England, it quoted Matthew 15:3, 6 like this:

"And why do you transgress the commandments of God for the sake of your traditions? . . . So for the sake of your traditions you have made void the word of God."

With such strong language the Lord firmly rejected the private doctrines and teachings of men.

But He promised a restoration of the truth—the whole truth! How could that be accomplished? And what do the other translators say about this great fact?

The New English Bible says that Jesus will not return "until the time of universal restoration comes."

Schoenfeld speaks of it as "the era of restoration."

Revised Version: "Whom heaven must receive until the time for the establishing of all that God spoke by the mouth of His holy prophets from of old."

Knox: "Then He will send out Jesus Christ who has now been made known unto you, but must have His dwelling place in Heaven until the time when all is restored anew."

The American Standard Version uses the expression "restoration of all things."

Twentieth Century: "The universal restoration."

Weymouth: "The re-constitution of all things."

So if we are willing to accept history and scripture, regardless of which Bible version we use, we must agree to two things:

1. The apostasy from the original Church was a stern reality.
2. A restoration of the whole gospel was promised.

But the questions next arise, when is this restoration to take place, and by what means will it come?

We turn to Revelation 14:6-7 and read:

"And I saw another angel fly in the midst of heaven, having the everlasting gospel to preach unto them that dwell on the earth, and to every nation, and kindred, and tongue, and people.

"Saying with a loud voice, Fear God, and give glory to him; for the hour of his judgment is come: and worship him that made heaven, and earth, and the sea, and the fountains of waters."

Lest anyone quibble about translations again we provide this:

New English Version: "I saw an angel flying in the mid-heaven with an eternal gospel (and of course there is only one [Ephesians 4:4-6]) to proclaim to those on earth, to every nation, and tribe, language and people. He cried with a loud voice, Fear God and pay homage to Him, for the hour of His judgment is come."

Standard Revised: "Then I saw another angel flying in mid-heaven with an eternal gospel to proclaim to those who dwell on earth."

Philips: "Then I saw another angel flying in mid-heaven holding the everlasting gospel to proclaim to the inhabitants of the earth. . . ."

Arendzen (Catholic): "And I saw another angel flying through the midst of heaven having the eternal gospel to preach. . . ."

Other versions teach the same doctrine, all making clear that an angel would restore the gospel. And when? In the hour of God's judgment, therefore a strictly modern event. And the church to be organized thereby would have to be a church of modern origin.

The old ones would not suffice.

And whose church would it be? As the Church of Jesus Christ, it had to bear His name.

To whom would the angel come?

Amos of the Old Testament said, "Surely the Lord God will do nothing but he revealeth his secret unto his servants the prophets." (Amos 3:7.)

That being the case, the angel would come only to a modern prophet and deliver the restored gospel to him.

All of this provides convincing identification of the true Church. To review, then, that Church would:

1. Acknowledge a universal apostasy in the past.

2. Be restored to earth by angelic ministry.

3. Carry the name of Jesus Christ.

4. Come in the hour of God's judgment.

5. Be a strictly modern institution.

6. Be organized with living apostles and prophets at the head.

7. Teach the gospel according to scripture and officiate in the true ordinances of Christ.

8. Have ministers who were called of God as was Aaron.

9. Enjoy current revelation.

Chapter Fourteen

A Marvelous Work

The Prophet Isaiah predicted the publication of a new volume of sacred writings as part of the restoration of the gospel.

Since this was to be a modern phenomenon to be accomplished by divine power, it would constitute unassailable identification of the true Church. Would any other group be made custodian of such a volume?

Just what did Isaiah say?

The prophecy appears in the twenty-ninth chapter of his book. It tells of a nation which was destroyed suddenly, its record to come from the ground, allowing that nation to "speak out of the dust."

The record was a sealed book. The words of the book would be delivered to a learned man with a request to "read this, I pray thee: and he saith, I cannot; for it is sealed:

"And the book is delivered to him that is not learned, saying, Read this, I pray thee: and he saith, I am not learned."

But through him this book would be published. "Wherefore the Lord said, Forasmuch as this people draw near me with their mouth, and with their lips do honour me, but have removed their heart far from me, and their fear toward me is taught by the precept of men:

"Therefore, behold, I will proceed to do a marvellous work among this people, even a marvellous work and a wonder: for the wisdom of their wise men shall perish, and the understanding of their prudent men shall be hid." (Isaiah 29:11-14.)

When was the book to appear? How do we know it would be modern?

The prophet provided a "deadline."

"Is it not yet a very little while, and Lebanon shall be turned into a fruitful field, and the fruitful field shall be esteemed as a forest?" (Isaiah 29:17.)

A definite time period can be established. Palestine had been a desolate and arid place for centuries. In 1917, during World War I, it was taken from Turkey by a British army under General Allenby. A short time later came the Balfour Declaration, and the United States and Great Britain sponsored the establishment of a homeland for the Jews.

As is well known, the nation of Israel has developed a vast reclamation project in the Holy Land. The Jews not only opened up large areas to agriculture with an irrigation system involving both the Jordan River and the Sea of Galilee, but they planted literally millions of trees throughout the valleys, and on the mountains as well.

Palestine is now a "fruitful field" as the scripture foresaw, and this has all evolved since 1917. But the book which Isaiah saw was destined to come forth before that happened; that is, before 1917!

"Is it not yet a very little while, and Lebanon shall be turned into a fruitful field, and the fruitful field shall be esteemed as a forest?"

The farms of Palestine are fruitful, the mountains are covered with forests, and the nation is exporting large volumes of fresh produce with its own fleet of merchant marine. The time has passed for the appearance of the promised book, its "deadline" expired.

Where is that book, and what is it like? We need to know because it will be an unmistakable mark by which to identify the true Church, for the Lord would not entrust this record to any other group. It will be with His prophets, without whom He does not act. (Amos 3:7.)

Ezekiel also spoke of the record in his thirty-seventh chapter. He did so as he foretold the gathering of Israel in the last days. He speaks of two "sticks," and allows these "sticks" to represent the nations of Judah and Ephraim which will be united eventually.

There will also be two records, one for Judah and one for Ephraim.

"Moreover, thou son of man, take thee one stick, and write upon it, For Judah, and for the children of Israel his companions: then take another stick, and write upon it, For Joseph, the stick of Ephraim, and for all the house of Israel his companions:

"And join them one to another into one stick; and they shall become one in thine hand." (Ezekiel 37:16-17.)

Then the prophet says that the Lord will take the stick or record of Ephraim and place it with the stick or record of Judah, and they will become one in His hands.

Similarly He will gather the tribes of Ephraim and Judah in the latter days, and will combine them into one as He does their histories.

"And when the children of thy people shall speak unto thee, saying, Wilt thou not shew us what thou meanest by these?

"Say unto them, Thus saith the Lord God; Behold, I will take the stick of Joseph, which is in the hand of Ephraim, and the tribes of Israel his fellows, and will put them with him, even with the stick of Judah, and make them one stick, and they shall be one in mine hand.

"And the sticks whereon thou writest shall be in thine hand before their eyes.

"And say unto them, Thus saith the Lord God; Behold, I will take the children of Israel from among the heathen, whither they be gone, and will gather them on every side, and bring them into their own land:

"And I will make them one nation in the land upon the mountains of Israel; and one king shall be king to them all: and they shall be no more two nations, neither shall they be divided into two kingdoms any more at all." (Ezekiel 37:18-22.)

The rest of the chapter refers further to the final restoration of the tribes of Israel.

What are those records? And where are they?

The record or "stick" of Judah is the Holy Bible. The record or "stick" of Ephraim is the book mentioned by Isaiah (Chapter 29) which would come out of the ground and provide the account of a people destroyed suddenly.

How do we know? By modern revelation!

It is important at this point that we bring together for joint consideration two of the most important passages in all scripture with respect to the modern work of the Lord.

One tells us of an angel who would fly from heaven to earth in the hour of God's judgment to restore the gospel. (Revelations 14:6-7.)

The other is a passage which has puzzled the scholars over the years, foretelling the coming forth of a sacred book "out of the ground" and "out of the dust" in the latter days. (Isaiah 29.) These two passages are closely related.

In ancient America two great nations lived side by side for a thousand years. They were frequently at war with each other. One nation consisted of dark-skinned people, the forefathers of the American Indian.

The other nation was white. Down through the centuries prophets of God ministered among both groups, even as the Hebrew prophets labored in Palestine.

These American prophets kept careful records of their own revelations, their sermons, their ordinances, and their general history. Having an abundance of metal available, they engraved their permanent records on thin sheets of gold which they bound together in book form.

About A.D. 400, toward the end of their thousand-year history, one of their prophets whose name was Mormon abridged the histories which had been written over ten centuries, and condensed them into one single volume. Hence, his work was known as the Book of Mormon, called after himself.

He had a son whose name was Moroni, also a prophet, who assisted his father in the final preparation of the abridged work.

Devastating warfare broke out again between these two peoples, and father and son fought side by side in defense of their families and their country. The father, Mormon, was killed, together with hundreds of thousands of other warriors. The final battle saw the complete annihilation of the white nation.

Moroni was left as the sole survivor of his people. He still possessed the golden record which his father had given him. It was the will of the Lord that it should be preserved until the latter days to be a means of converting both Jews and Gentiles to Christ.

Not only did the gold plates contain a thousand years of history and many revelations given by the Lord during that time, but it provided an account of the visit to America by the Savior following His resurrection in Palestine.

The Lord's miraculous appearance to those ancient Americans was described in detail. The record relates how Jesus showed the people the marks of the Crucifixion in His hands and feet and side. When they recognized Him, they bowed down and worshipped Him.

He preached His gospel to them, including the Sermon on the Mount. He taught them the doctrine of baptism and showed them how to baptize. He ordained twelve disciples and gave them power to officiate in these ordinances.

He healed their sick, blessed their children, and revealed to them the fulness of His gospel. Careful records were kept. As the people lived the gospel, they enjoyed peace and prosperity for 200 years. But at the end of that time, selfishness returned and men began to sin. Conditions steadily grew worse for another 200 years until the last great battle was fought with their enemies, and the white nation became extinct. Only Moroni survived.

About A.D. 420, under divine command, he encased the precious record containing the gospel in a box made of stone, and buried it in the ground for safekeeping.

It was the plan of God that this same Moroni would return to earth in the latter days as an angel to retrieve the record and make it available for publication to the world.

Now we begin to see the correlation between Isaiah's prophecy and that of John the Revelator. It was Moroni's record that Isaiah described. It contained the true gospel, just as the Lord Jesus Christ, His disciples, and the preceding prophets, had given it to the early Americans.

Since Moroni was the prophet who hid the record away, was he not the logical choice of the Lord to come back to earth and make it available for publication? Was not he—a prophet—fully worthy to be that angel, and was he not best equipped to bring forth his own volume?

The Lord so appointed him. He did fly through the midst of heaven in the hour of God's judgment as John said. He did fulfill the prophecy.

The volume literally contained the everlasting gospel. Its being made public would in fact "restore" the gospel. How else could this have been accomplished? How would an angel restore the gospel anyway? Could a conversation with someone on earth accomplish the task? Was not a sacred written record required?

Did not the Bible—the written scriptures of the Old World—provide gospel teachings for the ancients in that land? Moroni's book contained Christ's teachings in a similar way for the Western Hemisphere. Both books were scripture, both contained the word of God.

But the true meaning of the Bible was lost to the world as false doctrines were foisted upon the people who, in their ignorance, knew no better. The clergy rejected many of the Lord's doctrines and abolished or changed His ordinances.

For centuries no one was allowed even to read the Bible. One denomination denied all access to it by the people until recently.

With the Bible having lost its influence because so few read it and because of the changed liturgies of the churches, the people needed a new light to pierce the darkness which surrounded them. A second witness of Christ was required.

The Lord provided it from ancient America through Moroni who flew from the midst of heaven in the hour of God's judgment, came back to the hiding place of his record, delivering it to Joseph Smith who was raised up by the Almighty to be both translator and publisher of the book.

Moroni's record was undefiled and uncontaminated by the "wisdom of men." It contained the pure gospel of Christ and had been preserved by the hand of God for 1400 years to be brought forth in latter days for the salvation of all who would believe.

Its publication *restored* the gospel teachings to the earth in their purity. Moroni's people, who were "destroyed suddenly" in battle, now spoke "out of the ground" and "out of the dust" to people of our day.

So Moroni fulfilled the prophecies of both Isaiah and John the Revelator. Isaiah told about the book. Moroni produced it and delivered it to Joseph Smith who translated and published it in 1830.

The two prophecies came together in Moroni's mission. The word of God was vindicated. The new volume of scripture is the Book of Mormon.

By modern revelation the Lord tells us that He did in fact appoint Moroni to "reveal the Book of Mormon" in our day; that it does contain the fulness of the gospel, and that it is the record of the "stick" of Ephraim:

"Behold, this is wisdom in me; wherefore, marvel not, for the hour cometh that I will drink of the fruit of the vine with you on the earth, and with Moroni, whom I have sent unto you to reveal the Book of Mormon, containing the fulness of my everlasting gospel, to whom I have committed the keys of the record of the stick of Ephraim." (D & C 27:5.)

Although the Book of Mormon is rejected by many, to the Latter-day Saints it is indeed the sacred record spoken of by Isaiah, truly a marvelous work and a wonder as the ancient prophet said. And certainly it is one of the unmistakable marks of identification of the true Church.

None but the Latter-day Saints refer to these particular scriptures of Isaiah, Ezekiel, and John the Revelator in this manner. Who but the Latter-day Saints understand them?

Their fulfillment is part of the restoration of the gospel, and by following them, anyone with a desire to know may find the true Church of Jesus Christ.

Chapter Fifteen

A "Gathered" Church

When searching for the true Church of Jesus Christ, we must look for a church whose congregations have been "gathered" from many nations.

The scriptures indicate that when the gospel is restored it is to be taken to every nation, tongue, and people. It was the Lord who said:

"And this gospel of the kingdom shall be preached in all the world for a witness unto all nations; and then shall the end come." (Matthew 24:14.)

When John the Revelator told of the angel restoring the gospel in the last days he explained that the good word was to go to "every nation, and kindred, and tongue, and people." (Revelation 14:6.)

But although the gospel was thus to go worldwide, many Saints would be gathered from among the nations to a central place, which Isaiah described as being in the tops of the mountains. There they would build a temple. What church can fit into that pattern?

Both Isaiah and Micah spoke of the gathering to the tops of the mountains. Isaiah's prediction reads:

"And it shall come to pass in the last days, that the mountain of the Lord's house shall be established in the top of the mountains, and shall be exalted above the hills; and all nations shall flow unto it.

"And many people shall go and say, Come ye, and let us go up to the mountain of the Lord, to the house of the God of Jacob; and he will teach us of his ways, and we will walk in his paths: for out of Zion shall go forth the law, and the word of the Lord from Jerusalem.

"And he shall judge among the nations, and shall rebuke many people: and they shall beat their swords into plowshares, and their spears into pruninghooks: nation shall not lift up sword against nation, neither shall they learn war any more.

"O house of Jacob, come ye, and let us walk in the light of the Lord." (Isaiah 2:2-5. See also Micah 4:1-3.)

Making this even more clearly understood, some of the other Bible versions read as follows:

The Knox version:

"The Temple Hill! One day it shall stand there, highest of all the mountain heights, overtopping the peaks of them, and the nations will flock there together. A multitude of people will make their way to it, crying, Come let us climb up to the Lord's mountain peak, to the house where the God of Jacob dwells; He shall teach us the right way, we will walk in the paths He hath chosen." (Micah 4.)

The New World Translation:

"It must occur in the final part of the days, that the mountain of the house of Jehovah will become firmly established above the top of the mountains, and it will certainly be lifted up above the hills, and to it all nations must stream. And many people will certainly go and say, Come you people, let us go up to the mountain of Jehovah, to the House of the God of Jacob, and He will instruct us about His ways and we will walk in His paths." (Isaiah 2.)

This version presents Micah's declaration as follows: "And it must occur in the final part of the days that the mountain of the House of Jehovah will become firmly established above the top of the mountains, and it will certainly be lifted up above the hills, and to it people must stream. And many nations will certainly go and say, Come you people and let us go up to the mountain of Jehovah and to the House of the God of Jacob, and He will instruct us about His ways, and we will walk in His paths."

The Jerusalem Bible states the Micah version this way:

"In the days to come the mountain *of the temple* of Jehovah will be put on the top of the mountains and be lifted higher than the hills.

"The people will stream to it and they will say, Come, let us go to the mountain of Jehovah, *to the temple of the God of Jacob,* so that He may teach us of His ways and we will walk in His paths." (Italics added.)

In that Bible Isaiah reads as follows:

"In the days to come the mountain of the *temple of Jehovah* shall tower above the mountains and be lifted higher than the hills. All nations will stream to it. People without number will come to it and they will say, Come, let us go up to the mountain of Jehovah, to the *temple of the God of Jacob,* that He may teach us of His ways so that we may walk in His paths." (Italics added.)

Because so many of the early prophets were called to the high mountains to converse with God, mountains used for this purpose almost seemed like temples, so sacred were they to the ancient people.

It is interesting that both of these prophets would speak of a temple in connection with this gathering to the mountains. In fact, it is highly significant.

One of the chief reasons for the gathering of the Saints was to bring together enough manpower and financial strength to erect such structures. Temples were costly, beyond the ability of small congregations to build. But they were required by the Lord because some of the great saving ordinances were to be obtained there and in no other place.

So taught the Prophet Joseph Smith. The Saints were to gather from their homelands in those early days of the Church, travel to Zion and there build these temples, even in their poverty. Without the gathering there would not be sufficient population to meet this requirement of the Lord, for the Church was small in those days, and the people were scattered.

So it was that the Prophet Joseph Smith said that the main object of their gathering "was to build unto the Lord a house whereby He could reveal unto His people the ordinances of His house and the glories of His kingdom, and teach the people the way of salvation; for there are certain ordinances and principles that, when they are taught and practiced, must be done in a place or house built for that purpose.

"It was the design of the councils of heaven before the world was, that the principles and laws of the priesthood should be predicated upon the gathering of the people in every age of the world. Jesus did everything to gather the people, and they would not be gathered, and He therefore poured out curses upon them.

"Ordinances instituted in the heavens before the foundation of the world, in the priesthood, for the salvation of men, are not to be altered or changed. All must be saved on the same principles.

"It is for the same purpose that God gathers together His people in the last days, to build unto the Lord a house to prepare them for the ordinances and endowments, washings and anointings, etc.

"One of the ordinances of the house of the Lord is baptism for the dead. God decreed before the foundation of the world that that ordinance should be administered in a font prepared for that purpose in the house of the Lord. . . .

"If a man gets a fullness of the priesthood of God he has to get it in the same way that Jesus Christ obtained it, and that was by keeping all the commandments and obeying all the ordinances of the house of the Lord." (*Teachings of the Prophet Joseph Smith,* p. 308.)

When Malachi spoke of the second coming of Christ, and the messenger to be sent to prepare the way, he also said that "the Lord, whom ye seek, shall suddenly come to his temple." (Malachi 3:1.)

So there had to be a temple, and the "messenger" would have to be a temple builder.

Then we have these facts:

The restored gospel would be preached to all nations.

The latter-day Church would be a temple-building organization.

There would be a gathering of the scattered Saints for this purpose.

The Saints would assemble in the tops of the mountains.

There they would build a temple.

From there the gospel would be sent worldwide.

What church today can fit that pattern?

While Joseph Smith still lived, he built two temples, one at Kirtland and one at Nauvoo. He projected others, particularly at Independence, and Far West, Missouri.

A temple building prophet, his followers were a temple-building people.

They had literally "gathered" many from overseas, to Kirtland, Independence, and Nauvoo where temples were planned. So occurred such a gathering. And temple construction resulted.

Following the expulsion of the Saints from Nauvoo, and as part of their trek to the Great Basin, they planned for further temple construction.

A tremendous undertaking, the gathering to the "tops of the mountains" fulfilled the words of both Isaiah and Micah. It was by handcart and ox-cart, with thousands walking the entire distance of some two thousand miles from Nauvoo to the basin of the Great Salt Lake.

Before the coming of the railroad, 80,000 Saints traversed that route. They journeyed to the tops of the mountains, they built four temples in Utah in the pioneer period, and they sent missionaries to many parts of the world, as far away as Chile in South America, the South Sea Islands, and various countries in Europe, thus fulfilling the prophecy.

Later the gathering continued. There are now a million Latter-day Saints in the Utah area, with four million elsewhere in the United States, Canada, and eighty-seven other nations. The Church now grows by more than a million members every four or five years.

Thirty thousand missionaries are kept in the field laboring in those nations, teaching the gospel, and building up the Church. Now with five million of population, the effort is to build up the Church locally, and to stimulate that, the First Presidency is building temples in many convenient areas. Soon there will be forty-one in operation from Korea to Zurich.

The actual gathering movement predicted by Isaiah and Micah began in pioneer times, and the temples were constructed. We now see an expansion of the work in many nations worldwide, further identification of the true Church.

Chapter Sixteen

The Fulfillment

The Church of Jesus Christ would fit its biblical description in any period of history, if it were on the earth at all. The Lord is unchangeable, His gospel is the same. It is the everlasting gospel, the everlasting covenant.

The conditions of salvation never alter, and no man on earth has the right to make changes suitable to himself. God's ways are not man's ways.

Christ is not inconsistent or variable over the ages, neither is His Church, in organization, in doctrine, or in its ordinances. Therefore, the signs of identification by which it may readily be recognized would be the same always.

When Paul wrote the Ephesians about "one Lord, one faith (or gospel), one baptism" (Ephesians 4:5), his remarks were as applicable to modern times as they were to ancient times.

This volume has attempted to list some of the signs of the true Church. There are others as well. Those given are exact identification, they are scriptural, and they point with unerring accuracy to only one church on earth at the present time. That is The Church of Jesus Christ of Latter-day Saints.

All the signs of identification listed in this book apply directly and exactly to the so-called "Mormon" Church and to none other. These marks are unique for the most part.

If there are some denominations which may have one or another of these marks, such, for example, as immersion baptism, they would still be incomplete. As the Apostle Paul said, all parts of the body must be present, and all must be "fitly joined together."

The testimony of history, the testimony of scripture, the testimony of modern revelation all affirm that The Church of Jesus Christ of Latter-day Saints, with headquarters in Salt Lake City, Utah, is that true Church, the only one on earth with which the Lord is well pleased, as He said Himself. (D & C 1:30.)

Such is the testimony of this book, and such is the testimony of five million members in some eighty-seven nations, who unitedly declare that:

God is our Eternal Father, and He lives.

Jesus Christ of Nazareth is our Savior and our Redeemer.

Joseph Smith was His prophet through whom the gospel was restored in these latter days.

The Book of Mormon is true and sustains the Bible in fact.

The priesthood is on earth today in this Church as it was in the time of Peter and Paul.

Prophets preside in this Church guided by current revelation, for "surely the Lord God will do nothing, but he revealeth his secret unto his servants the prophets." (Amos 3:7.)

As a mighty legacy to the world, the Prophet Joseph Smith gave this testimony of the Lord Jesus Christ:

"And now, after the many testimonies which have been given of him, this is the testimony, last of all, which we give of him: That he lives!

"For we saw him, even on the right hand of God; and we heard the voice bearing record that he is the Only Begotten of the Father—

"That by him, and through him, and of him, the worlds are and were created, and the inhabitants thereof are begotten sons and daughters unto God." (D & C 76:22-24.)